Be the *best*
Best Man and make
a stunning speech!

Practical books that inspire

Making a Wedding Speech
How to face the big occasion with confidence and style

Making the Bridgegroom's Speech
Know what to say, when to say it and enjoy the big day

Making the Father of the Bride's Speech
*Be positive, humorous and sensitive and deliver
a memorable speech*

Stand and Deliver
Leave them stirred not shaken

2-4-6-8 How Do You Communicate?
How to make your point in just a minute

howtobooks

Please send for a free copy of the latest catalogue:

How To Books
3 Newtec Place, Magdalen Road,
Oxford OX4 1RE, United Kingdom
email: info@howtobooks.co.uk
http://www.howtobooks.co.uk

Be the *best*
Best Man and make
a stunning speech!

Phillip Khan-Panni

howtobooks

Other books by Phillip Khan-Panni

2-4-6-8 How Do You Communicate?
Blank Page to First Draft in 15 Minutes
Stand & Deliver: Leave them stirred not shaken

Published by How To Books Ltd,
3 Newtec Place, Magdalen Road,
Oxford OX4 1RE. United Kingdom.
Tel: (01865) 793806. Fax: (01865) 248780.
email: info@howtobooks.co.uk
http://www.howtobooks.co.uk

British Library Cataloguing in Publication Data
A catalogue record for this book is available from the British
Library

Cover design by Baseline Arts Ltd, Oxford
Produced for How To Books by Deer Park Productions
Typeset by PDQ Typesetting, Newcastle-under-Lyme, Staffs.
Printed and bound by Cromwell Press, Trowbridge, Wiltshire.

NOTE: The material contained in this book is set out in good
faith for general guidance and no liability can be accepted
for loss or expense incurred as a result of relying in particular
circumstances on statements made in the book. The laws and
regulations are complex and liable to change, and readers should
check the current position with the relevant authorities before
making personal arrangements.

Contents

Preface   9

1.   Your Complete Guide to Being Best Man   13

*As you face the terror of the realisation that you have
agreed to be best man at a friend's wedding, you wonder
where you will find all the answers to your questions, and
the help to do a great job. The answer is: in this book.
This chapter sets out to reassure you, and gives you the
background to many of the customs and rituals of
western weddings.*

2.   Myths and Legends   22

*Not only myths and legends concerning weddings, but
superstitions too! Why do grooms carry their brides
over the threshold? Why do women propose on Leap
Year day? What's the role of flowers in foretelling the
future? Why do children tie the churchyard gate shut?
What's the origin of the wedding day races? And what
about such quaint customs as bundling and throwing the
stocking. It's all explained in this chapter.*

3.   Duties of the Best Man   31

*Before you go much further, you'll want to know what's
expected of you, and why your role is so important to the
success of the wedding day. This chapter gives you a
checklist of your responsibilities, and helps you realise
why the groom will depend so heavily on you. This will
help you understand how to be a cracking master of
ceremonies and make a superb impression. The speech
comes next.*

4.   Planning Your Speech   45

*Probably the greatest cause for concern is the best man's
speech. It may be a short interlude in your life, but it is
a pivotal one that needs careful planning. Here's your
essential guide to researching the material for your*

*speech – whom to talk to, what to ask, what kind of
props you might gather to make your speech memorable.*

5.   Preparation   **54**

*You are going to get a lot of good advice in this book.
Here you'll get reassurance about what you already
know, plus ten key points to form a framework in your
mind for the things you'll have to do as best man. This
chapter is like the foundation of the edifice of activities
that will grow as you approach the wedding day.*

6.   Writing the Speech in Eight Steps   **61**

*Starting with your ten key points, this chapter gives you
the simplest and easiest route to getting your speech
together. The process it describes is ideal for preparing
any speech or presentation, whether for a social occasion
or for business. It will remove the stress of starting with
a blank sheet of paper, and guide you to arriving at a
speech that others will want to hear.*

7.   Things to Avoid   **72**

*Everyone wants you to succeed, and so do you. It is
important not to let yourself down by saying or doing the
wrong thing. This chapter reminds you of some of the
pitfalls that await the unwary: topics and attitudes to
avoid in your speech, guidance on rude jokes, and
unacceptable language, and even words of warning about
the right way to conduct yourself. This is the Dutch
Uncle slot.*

8.   The Big Day   **79**

*This chapter brings together all the ideas,
responsibilities and reminders you will need when the big
day finally arrives. It summarises all that you need to
know and remember, helps you to prepare yourself in
your mind, gives you 20 top tips and provides a checklist
to help you ensure that you have covered all the bases.*

9. Delivery 97

OK, you've researched and prepared your speech, sweated blood over writing a draft, and now it's time to consider how to put it across. Should you bury your head in A4 pages and read the speech? How do you get your heart and shaking limbs under control? This chapter gives you a short cut to the speaking secrets of professional speakers, to help you sound better than you may have thought possible.

10. Anecdotes 109

Often you can pass on wisdom through stories, and this chapter offers you a range of anecdotes, some serious, some amusing, some just plain silly. Use them as they stand or adapt them to suit the occasion. Or read them just to put you in the mood, when you start to write your speech.

11. Jokes and Quotes 119

No book on the best man's speech would be complete without a selection of quips and quotes. Most of them are one-liners, all of them are brief. These have been gathered from numerous sources. Some jokes are from real life, others have been adapted from jokes on the internet and elsewhere, while the quotable quotes have been selected for their relevance to weddings.

12. Traditional and Celebrity Sayings 136

Ireland has been a rich source of wisdom and paradox, and of sentimentality too. Celebrities, past and present, have also contributed to the treasure trove of aphorisms about relationships and marriage. They range from the openly cynical to the deeply lovelorn, and there will be something to fit the mood of your speech as well.

13. Sample Toasts: Beginnings, Middles and Endings 147

How did the custom of toasting begin? How to do it right? Find the answers in this chapter. Plus several beginnings, middles and endings, to let you mix and match. They are not only templates, but samples of mini speeches that will suit many occasions.

14. Mixed Marriages   155
Some mixed marriages do not follow the western pattern, and do not require a best man. They have therefore been excluded from this chapter, and from this book. However, even in informal marriages between people from different cultures, some sensitivity is called for. In this chapter you'll find a couple of sample speeches for such occasions.

Sample Speech 1   161
This is the first of several full length speeches, to illustrate how to bring in stories about the groom's early days, how he and his bride met, and your role in the mix.

Sample Speech 2   167
This sample speech focuses on the development of the relationship between the groom and the best man, giving an insight into the groom's bachelor ways, and how, at last, he met his Waterloo.

Sample Speech 3   173
This is a speech for the wedding of a trader on the stock exchange, to provide an example of how to develop the background of a high-powered person. It concludes with a toast to the two families that are being brought together by the wedding.

Sample Speech 4   178
When the best man was a woman. This is the actual speech given by Evelyn Ryan when she was the best man. It may be rare but, increasingly, women are being awarded the role of best man. And why not?

Index   183

Preface

Being best man at a wedding is more than having to 'say a few words'. In fact, I doubt anyone is ever given such a casual brief for such an important task, unless the groom neither knows nor cares about the significance of his own wedding day. Marriage may not be as popular today as it was even thirty years ago, but it still happens all the time. And blokes still get asked to be best man. And they still say 'Yes'.

When I got married in the 1960s, my brother was my best man. He hadn't a clue how to do the job, because there was no one to tell him. Curiously enough, the situation today is not much better. There are books a-plenty about wedding speeches, and guidance for the groom and the father of the bride. Yet the poor best man, whose role is so pivotal in the matrimonial celebrations, gets very little help. Hence this book.

When I started to write it, my focus was on the brief but terrifying prospect: The Speech. After all, that's my speciality. I've probably won more speech contests than anyone in Britain and Ireland, so I have faced and endured the dread of public failure more often than most. Yet even I would approach a best man's speech with trepidation. So, of course, I started to write about the technique of assembling a speech and getting that terror under control, employing the tools of a professional speechmaker.

However, as I researched the subject, I was struck by the rich history behind the best man's role, and by the wealth of ancient rituals and superstitions that have fashioned the wedding ceremony and its attendant celebrations. Many have long since been forgotten, except in sayings that have as little meaning as 'Bless you!' when someone sneezes.

I thought I should bring some of that back, without losing sight of my main purpose, which was to help the best man cope with his heavy responsibilities. In addition, I wanted to imbue you with excitement, when you are best man – excitement about the whole wedding process. I wanted to find stories to share with you, and suitable jokes and quotations that would lift your speech well above the bare necessities, and provide you with a good read along the way.

This book was the result.

I want you to be more than a good best man. I want you to be the very *best* best man you can be, and make the very *best* best man's speech that they will have ever heard. It will honour your mate, the groom, and it will pay respect to his chosen bride. It will sharpen your own profile too.

One new development was the realisation that these days women are sometimes given the job of best man. One of my closest friends, Evelyn Ryan, was one of these, and I have included her speech as sample speech 4. So to any woman who happens to be reading this for guidance, let me offer my apologies for referring to the best man always in the masculine gender. The same considerations apply to you, except for attire. The female best man should match what the bride is wearing, but be careful not to dress more strikingly than her. It is, after all, her big day.

So, finally, what's this book about? It started out as a guide to the best man's speech. It grew into a one-stop guide to being a really effective best man. It includes background information to position your thinking, and checklists to help you organize your actions. Above all, its purpose is to help you to enjoy your role as best man, and to make it a memorable occasion for the bride and groom.

Phillip Khan-Panni

To June
who was my wife and my best friend,
and who showed me by her example
what it means to love, honour
and respect your partner within a marriage.

CHAPTER 1

Your Complete Guide to Being Best Man

Why this book?

So your friend is getting married and he has asked you to be best man at the wedding. And you accepted. Now the doubts creep in and the terror begins. Where do you turn for advice? Who can guide you in your duties? And above all, who will help you with the all-important speech?

This book is the answer to all your questions.

In it you will find everything you need to know about your role in the wedding ceremony and the reception. It will tell you about the background to, and origins of, the rituals that attend the joining together of a man and woman in matrimony. It will explain why there is a best man, why the bride stands on the left, what the best man's duties are and why. It will also give you an insight into the wedding practices of different communities in Britain and elsewhere.

It includes a simple guide to the etiquette involved, and to making sure that the planning is painless and nothing important is overlooked.

What it will do for you

It will guide you in the preparation of your speech, and in

delivering it with style and panache. Finally, it contains **examples of best man speeches** for a number of different scenarios, including 'When the Best Man was a Woman'. You may adapt them to suit your own needs.

In short, this book provides you with everything you need to *be* the best best man and to make the very *best* best man's speech.

There are other books on the planning and etiquette of weddings, and even books on making wedding speeches. They tend to be packed with jokes, anecdotes and examples of short speeches, but very little on how to go about preparing and delivering a speech that will make an impact. In this book I have sought to remedy that, while not forgetting to provide a wealth of reference material.

There are jokes, there are anecdotes, and there are sample speeches, both short and long. The long speeches are towards the back, and they are examples of 'real' speeches, lasting 10-15 minutes each. In Chapter 14, I give you some examples of toasts that are mini speeches. In fact, you can mix and match from the examples in that chapter. For most people, and for most weddings, a short speech will be what's required, but don't feel you *must* limit yourself to four or five minutes. Once you are in full flow, you may find that it's going really well and you are enjoying yourself. No one will be putting a stopwatch on your speech, and nor should you.

The guiding principle is to stop before your audience wants you to. Always leave them wanting more. Never make them want *less*!

You can make a great impression

The purpose of this book is to enable you to use the occasion to develop some speechmaking skills. Making a public speech is hard. Making a good one is even harder. Most people are glad to get a giggle or two, then get it done and get off the stage, so to speak, thankful that they may never have to face the ordeal again. But isn't it a shame to waste the opportunity to make something more of the opportunity?

If you make a brilliant best man speech you will benefit in a number of ways:

◆ You will benefit directly by impressing those present, especially those who never suspected your ability to command an audience.

◆ It will give you a degree of self-confidence you may never have thought possible.

◆ And it will open the way to progress in your working life, where good communication skills are increasingly valued.

Think about the people you most admire, both in your private life and in the business arena. What do they have in common? That's right, it's *the ability to put their points across* in a way that makes others want to listen and act. *You* could be like them. Of course, this book will help you if all you want to do is to make an acceptable best man speech and hope you'll never be asked again. In fact, if you follow the guidelines and checklists you will be much better than acceptable.

However, if you would like to develop as a speaker, this book will help you to achieve that goal. It will do more. It will help you to run the wedding efficiently. As best man you will be in charge, and you'll have to make decisions, take initiatives and look after people and things at a level you may never have done before. It's not difficult, nor particularly onerous, so long as you know what to do.

This book will guide you every step of the way. Towards the end there is a chapter summarising what you need to think about and do on the wedding day itself. It's a checklist for the day. Once you have read the book, it would be worth copying the chapter and carrying it with you, especially on the wedding day.

Once upon a time

Weddings are full of traditions. The ceremonies them-selves are relatively recent in their origins, dating from the establishment of Christianity in Europe, but *many of the rituals are centuries older*. It's worth reminding ourselves of the origins of the customs that we still follow in traditional wedding ceremonies.

How the role of best man evolved

Starting with the basics, consider the practice of **asking the bride's parents** for her hand in marriage. It was not always so. If we look back only a few hundred years we will see that a man did not seek permission to marry the girl he wanted. He didn't ask her parents and he didn't ask her. He simply *kidnapped* her from her village and carted her off to his own. On the way home the groom kept his captured bride on his left because he was likely to have been right handed, and he need his right arm free to wield a sword or some other weapon.

He did not always go alone. He usually went *with a close friend*, whose role was to help the groom fight off her family and/or any friends or rival suitors who might come in pursuit. More often than not, the groom went mob-handed, and his raiding party were known as **groomsmen**. They were usually a group of young bachelors for whom such raids were the highlights of the year.

By the nineteenth century, however, the groomsmen had acquired respectable status, and their role was that of **ceremonial attendants**. The special friend who was appointed **best man** was by then chosen more for his close friendship than for his long sword arm. He was given the tasks of paying the priest and safeguarding the ring, which the groom was deemed likely to lose in the stress of the occasion, and generally looking after things like a **master of ceremonies.**

The bridesmaids

The best man speaks for the **bridesmaids** or matron of honour, but their role pre-dates his by many centuries. In fact, bridesmaids were considered absolutely essential by the **ancient Egyptians**. It was their belief that mischievous spirits were likely to spoil the party by the use of trickery and black magic, simply out of spite.

To thwart those spirits, and avoid the possibility of *an unwelcome intervention* on the happy day, to say nothing of the dismay that would be felt if the bride were to *be abducted for a second time*, several young ladies were dressed up as extravagantly as the bride herself, so that any passing evil spirit would be unable to decide which was the bride, and they would proceed on their way without causing trouble.

The wedding cake

The ancient Egyptians also gave us the **wedding cake**, although its original significance has largely been forgotten. A modern best man might joke that 'even the wedding cake is in tiers', but he's closer to the truth than he might realise.

The Egyptian wedding cake was originally of barley or wheat. During the wedding ceremony the cake was broken over the head of the bride, either to signify fertility or to ensure it. Sometimes it caused her some pain, so that some people (much later) referred to it as the '**headache cake**'. Strangely, the Egyptians did not eat the cake, although as time progressed it evolved into a towering, multi-tiered creation, much as we have today. The bride and groom had to kiss over the top of the large cake, and it was considered good fortune if they managed to do so without knocking it over.

During the reign of England's King Edward II, the symbolic cake became an edible one, possibly because the population at large could not afford to waste any potential food. To make the cake even more appealing, it became the practice to ice the cake, and for every guest to eat a piece. Indeed, it was considered lucky to share in the cake, as though the eating of a morsel reinforced the good wishes and hopes for future happiness.

The wedding ring and the bride's veil

Let's now consider the **wedding ring** and the **bride's veil.** Here we have to thank the **Romans.** They were the ones who first started wearing the wedding ring on the third finger of the left hand, because they believed that this finger carries a vein that connects directly with the heart. The Romans weren't only conquering soldiers, they were romantic souls as well.

But why the left hand? Because the right hand was used for the household chores, and would therefore get dirtier. The left hand remained relatively clean, and was therefore the more pleasant location for the symbol of love. Also, the wedding ring was less likely to get scratched on the less active left hand.

The custom of *wearing a veil* may have originated in the East, but one source attributes it to the Romans, who frequently had arranged marriages. The bride wore a veil so that the husband would not see his bride's face until the wedding was over, in case he thought her too ugly and decided not to go through with the wedding. Today it symbolises something much healthier – when the bride throws back her veil she is telling her new husband that she is now his, without hindrance.

Tying shoes to the back of the car

The Romans developed yet another ancient Egyptian wedding custom: the custom that has now evolved into **tying shoes** to the back of the car that drives the newlyweds away.

It began with the Egyptians. They habitually *swapped sandals* when a deal was done, to signify the transfer of ownership. So when a girl married, her father handed her sandals to her new husband, thereby *transferring ownership* to the groom. The custom survived for centuries, until the Romans modified it. Roman grooms would tap their brides' shoes, and guests would shower the couple with shoes at the close of the wedding ceremony.

In 1860, at a Leicestershire village wedding, the bride's brother found a **battered hobnailed boot** in the road and he threw it over the bride and groom. It landed in the rhododendrons beyond, and the bridesmaids all rushed to claim it, for she who won it would soon be wed. The lucky winner hung the boot in her house, from a white ribbon, until the day she married.

These days it is more usual to **throw rice**. However, that's an ancient practice too, dating from pagan times, when grain was thrown over the bride to shower her with fertility. In Nottinghamshire, wheat was thrown, accompanied by the cry, *'Bread for life and pudding for ever!'*

Those are the origins of the more common traditions, but there are quite a few more, including several potent superstitions, which I will detail in the next chapter.

CHAPTER 2

Myths and Legends

This chapter is not strictly about the duties of the best man, but when you are thinking about a wedding, it could be of interest to know about some old **traditions and superstitions**. They might even be useful thoughts to include in the speech. Certainly they explain some of the customs that still prevail in particular parts of the English-speaking world.

The threshold

Take the practice of **carrying the bride across the threshold**, for example. To understand this you need to go back to the origin of the threshold itself. In ancient times, most houses had mud floors which would get slippery and messy from the rain water that was carried in on the shoes and boots of people going in and out of the house. To counter this, straw (thresh) was laid on the floor. Inevitably, the thresh would spread and creep through the doorway, so a wooden bar was laid across the doorway to hold back the thresh, hence *threshold*.

On entering her new home, the bride had to be careful not to trip or stumble on the threshold, as that was a bad omen, signifying that the marriage itself would fail. To avoid this, the groom would pick up his bride and carry her safely over the threshold. It apparently did not matter if he tripped on his own threshold. Of course, there were dangers, as when the bride was heavier than the groom, and it could be that some negotiation had to take place. So the practice of carrying the bride over the threshold was by no means either obligatory or universal. However, it did add a gallant touch to the end of a wonderful day.

Women proposing

There were a number of interesting ways in which marriages were made. In the Middle Ages, in England, although women had far fewer rights than men, they could propose on **February 29th** – Leap Year Day – because that was not an official day on the calendar. Therefore, no laws applied, and women were free of the restrictions that governed their behaviour the rest of the year. They seized the opportunity to resolve relationships that were taking too long to lead to marriage and to push indecisive suitors into action.

More commonly, especially in rural areas, a girl would peel an apple in a single paring and throw the skin over her shoulder, hoping it would land in the shape of the initial letter of her lover's name. This practice of **apple paring** was carried over to North America by the pioneers, whose young women held group apple paring ceremonies to discover whom they should wed.

Flowers to divine the future

Flowers played an important role in such **divination**. Apart from the ever popular rose, the succulent **orpine** was used to determine a lover's fidelity. In England the plant is called 'Livelong', because it remains fresh long after plucking. A girl would pluck an orpine on Midsummer's Eve and stick it on her doorpost. The next morning she would hurry to see which way it had inclined overnight: to the right meant her lover was faithful. The other way was bad news.

On **Midsummer's Day**, in the West Country, a girl would pick a **rose** and place it in white paper to preserve its colour. If she wore the rose to church on Christmas Day, her future husband would reveal himself by silently taking it from her.

Hydrangeas, especially blue ones, were considered *unlucky* if grown too near the house, because while they flowered, daughters would not wed. **Myrtle** figures in folk songs about love and marriage. It was used in bridal bouquets, and it was the custom for a bridesmaid to take a sprig from the bouquet and plant it, when the wedding party returned from the church. If the sprig took, it signified happiness for the newlyweds, and an early marriage for the bridesmaid who did the planting.

It has long been a tradition for bridal parties, especially in rural areas, to walk to church along a **flower-strewn**

path. Marigolds, rosemary, marsh iris, rushes and wheat have also been used to add symbolism as well as perfume to the bride's last few steps as a single woman. Sometimes she would be halted if the clock was about to strike, as it was considered unlucky if the clock chimed during the wedding. Perhaps for this reason bridal parties in some areas would circle the church three times, going east to west, before entering the church.

Old English traditions

There is an assortment of other traditions to follow the wedding ceremony. A common one is the requirement that *the clergyman should kiss the bride*. Indeed, sometimes the vicar would find the newlyweds waiting patiently for him to fulfil their expectations.

In **Chaddleworth**, Berkshire, there is a steep step at the church door, and it is said that whoever first steps over it on the way out will remain master of the household ever after. This has led, at times, to a race to the line by bride and groom! Outside, in parts of the west country children would tie the churchyard gate shut, and open it only after the groom had thrown them some money – perhaps a task for the best man to manage.

In **Cleveland**, the bride and groom would mark the ending of their single lives by *leaping over a bench*, while a gun loaded with feathers was fired into the air, as an expression of the hope that nothing harder would ever fall on the newlyweds.

Races for the young men

To this day it is quite common for the bride, at her reception, to raise her skirt and remove a **ceremonial garter** from the top of her white stocking. It has a clearly sexual meaning, and originated in north country weddings, where the garter was removed by wedding guests who raced to be the first to do so as soon as the bride had been taken home to be bedded. The young swains would leap on their horses and race to the bride's new home, where the winner would kneel at the doorway, awaiting the bride's arrival. She would raise her skirt and allow him to remove it, sometimes with his teeth, encouraging him to hand it to his own sweetheart for good fortune in love. In time, the race to remove the garter was advanced to the church itself, resulting in unseemly behaviour at the altar, so the custom was modified to offer the garter from the bride's bosom, and even to replace it with a ribbon.

There were other wedding races, which made country weddings incredibly rowdy. One was **Riding for the Kale**, which was a spiced broth of cabbage. The chase was more important than the prize, although contestants would often line up before the race for a kiss from the bride. In the North of England, they would race their horses wildly, and fire their guns, as a reminder of the days when the bride was captured.

In the Midlands, right until the 18th century, they would **race for the wedding cake**. The cake was placed on a 12 foot pole, and the young men would gallop their horses to be the first to knock the cake down. Pieces of the cake were then *passed through the wedding ring* and given to unmarried women to place under their pillows, to encourage dreams of the men they would eventually marry.

Fertility rites

Elsewhere, such as Sussex, every wedding featured a 'bride's pie', which consisted of a baked hen stuffed full of hard-boiled eggs and covered with a thick crust. The pie was to bring the newlyweds good luck and many children.

These days, it is the norm for the bride to **throw the bridal bouquet** towards the bridesmaids and other female guests. The one to catch it is supposed to be the next to wed. That practice was pre-dated by two other customs. One was called 'throwing the stocking'. After the couple had retired to bed, the wedding party would noisily stamp up the stairs to their bedroom and sit at the foot of the bed. The guests, male and female, would pick up the bride's stockings and throw them over their shoulders. Early pregnancy was supposed to follow if a stocking thrown by a man fell on the bride, or if one thrown by a woman fell on the groom.

The other custom was the **drinking of the sack posset** at the end of the wedding feast. This was a drink of hot, sweetened milk curdled with the addition of sack, a strong wine that was imported from Spain and the Canary Islands in the 16th and 17th centuries. The wedding ring was dropped in the posset and whoever found it would be the next to marry.

Courting

One of the more intriguing courtship practices was that of 'bundling'. A courting couple would sleep in the same bed, fully dressed, and with a plank of wood separating them, down the middle of the bed. Originating in Wales, this custom was adopted and maintained by the Pennsylvania Dutch and in parts of Canada right into the mid-19th century. When one preacher protested about the propriety of the custom, he was told, 'You wouldn't buy a horse without first sitting astride it to see how it trotted.'

In areas where bundling was prevalent, mothers would preserve their daughters' virtue by giving them **courting stockings**, which were meant to contain both legs together, like a mermaid.

Green stockings had a ritual role for men. If a farmer's younger son married before his elder brother, the latter had to wear green stockings and dance in the pigs' trough, to avert bad luck.

Prosperity, fine weather and a popular saying

Among the other popular traditions was the practice of putting **a sixpence in the bride's shoe**, although that would be hard for the younger generation to understand as the sixpence no longer exists. However, it was the Romans, two thousand years ago, who started the practice of putting a small silver coin in the bride's shoe, to bring her wealth and prosperity.

In Ireland they put the **Infant of Prague** statuette outside the door the night before the wedding to ensure good weather for the event.

Finally, remember the saying,'Something old, something new, something borrowed, something blue'?

- **Something old** signifies the past life the bride is leaving behind, but not forgotten altogether.

- **Something new** points to the new life she is about to begin, and the good fortune it is supposed to bring.

- **Something borrowed** from a happily married woman means the new bride will enjoy similar happiness and luck in her own marriage.

◆ **Something blue** refers to the traditional colour to
signify purity. Blue was worn for weddings from
biblical times until Queen Victoria's time. She was
the one who introduced white as the symbol of
purity.

CHAPTER 3

Duties of the Best Man

The **role** of the best man is pivotal in making the wedding day a success. Whether the occasion is formal or informal, there are **arrangements** to be made, **rituals** to be observed, **courtesies** to be extended, and the groom's hand to be held.

If you are the best man, that's your job. All of the above. Plus a very important speech that everyone is looking forward to hearing.

A groom I know had an altogether too casual approach to his own wedding and when his best man asked him what he should do, the groom just said, 'Turn up and be funny.' In saying that, he was doing his best man a great disservice and placing him in peril.

Imagine this: as best man you are expecting to just turn up on the wedding day and string together half a dozen jokes that you've picked up in the pub or from the internet. Two days before the event *you suddenly realise that the groom has ordered a morning suit* for himself, assuming that you would know enough to order one for yourself. You hurriedly ring all the numbers in *Yellow Pages*, only to discover that there's a garden party at Buckingham Palace that weekend, and all the morning suits have been hired out already.

Then you learn that *the guest list is 100 strong,* full of people you don't know, and not just the half dozen mates that you'd been led to expect. Now you know that you will have to make a speech and act as master of ceremonies. In a lounge suit.

No, it doesn't bear thinking about, although I've known such a scenario actually to occur.

You consider your options:

1. Emigrate.
2. Abdicate.
3. Communicate.

Option 1 is not on, and Option 2 depends on finding a suitable alternative candidate. Also, the groom will never speak to you again, and you might mind that, even though he has landed you in the soup. So you have got to *communicate.* The question is, with whom?

If you are reading this, you have found the answer.

Let me start by giving you a **checklist of your responsibilities**, then expand on them. I shall deal with **the speech** separately.

The first thing to realise is that there is no standard procedure. Certain elements of the best man's duties are universal, but there are significant differences between

Britain and the USA, and other differences in Ireland. However, there are broadly three sets of duties:

1. General planning.
2. Being MC on the day.
3. At the reception.

If you are at ease with the administrative side of things, you can skip to item 3, or proceed to the next chapter and get on with preparing your speech.

1. General planning

This includes all the long-range planning that the bride and groom will probably take care of, but you need to stick your oar in and make sure they do not forget anything significant.

◆ **Brief the caterer**.
It will not be your responsibility to deal with the catering itself, as that is the preserve of the bride's father. However, you are responsible for managing the party and also for the speeches (including your own). You therefore need to have an understanding with the caterer to ensure that the tables are cleared and relative silence restored before the speeches begin. The clatter of crockery is irritating to the guests as well to the speakers.

◆ **Order the buttonhole carnations for key people**.
Find out early who is arranging flowers for the
occasion (bride's bouquet and anything else) and
offer to deal directly with the florist for buttonhole
carnations for the key people, i.e. the groom, the
bride's father, yourself, the ushers.

◆ **Book the car(s) and get a written confirmation**.
Car hire people, especially in the busy periods, will
tend to be unreliable, and could easily let you
down. Never take a verbal acceptance or
confirmation from them. Oh, by the way, did I
mention that you should **never take a verbal
acceptance or confirmation**? Make sure the (written)
contract is for **all** the necessary journeys. Some car
hire people have been known to try and do two
overlapping weddings in the same morning, only to
be held up while returning from the second one,
leaving the first wedding party hanging around at
the church. They have then offered to charge only
for the first journey, even though they had actually
broken the contract by not being there for the
return trip.

◆ **Reserve the formal attire (if appropriate)**.
It's up to the bride and groom if they want to have
a formal wedding, with morning suits and perhaps
even top hats. Ask what they want, then make
arrangements right away to book the outfits for the
groom, for yourself and for anyone else who needs

to be dressed formally, such as ushers, groomsmen and the bride's father. Ideally, hire all from the same shop so that everyone will look the same. And don't wait. Even Moss Bros doesn't have unlimited stocks, and you cannot count on the suits being available if you book late. If it is not going to be formal you should still ensure that all ushers wear a similar suit to your own, e.g. all in black or navy or grey, all with matching ties, shirts and shoes.

♦ **Talk to the disco DJ or the leader of the band about the order of events and the choice of music.**
Will it be live music or a disco? Make an early decision and make the booking, but only after interviewing and auditioning the DJ or band leader. Then ask for a play list. If they are to start playing music during the meal, what kind of music do you want then? What mix of dance music for later? Work out the complete programme, including where and for how long the breaks will be. You will need to give some indication of the kind of guests you will be expecting. Will it be ancient relatives from the far flung corners of the globe or rowdies from the rugby club, Dad's Army or Chancers from The Square Mile? Remember the three rules for booking such services:
1. Never pay fully in advance.
2. Never pay fully in advance.
3. Never pay fully in advance.

◆ **Check with the clergyman or register office on the timetable**.
Never forget that your mate's wedding may not be the only one that day, and although you may not be making the arrangements (that's what the groom and the bride's father will be doing) you will be the **sergeant-major** on the wedding day, the one responsible for keeping to the **agreed time-table** for getting there, for the completion of the ceremony, for the **photo shoot** afterwards, and for getting away for the reception.

◆ **Find out who needs to be paid, how much and when**.
Agree in advance with the groom and the bride's father who needs paying and who will do the paying. Most probably it will all be taken care of in advance, but be prepared to make last-minute payments.

◆ **Organise the team of ushers or groomsmen**. You can't do everything, so share the load with a hand-picked team. Their roles will not be onerous: mainly to guide wedding guests to their places and help sort out simple problems or answer questions. Guests need to know whom they should ask if they need anything, even if it's only to know where the toilets are, or to identify themselves as the vegetarians.

◆ **Draw up a guest list for the church/register office**.
This is not strictly necessary, but it may help in

planning a balanced look, especially if there are many more expected on the bride's side than on the groom's, or vice versa. Also, it impresses the hell out of guests to know that they are expected, with their names on a printed list.

♦ **Ensure that the bride's father draws a table plan for the sit-down meal.**
This makes for an efficient start to the meal, and it is a good idea to mark on the plan who are the **vegetarians**, and have a coloured sticker on the back of those chairs so the waiters/waitresses don't have to keep asking. In addition, if you have ever been to a formal dinner with a table plan, you will notice that people spend an unnecessarily long time looking at their names on the table plan. They love it! And they like to see who else will be on their table.

♦ **Research your speech by talking to the parents, siblings, friends, colleagues.**
Parents can give you the best insights, as well as photographs and/or other mementoes of notable moments that you may wish to mention in your speech. Siblings can tell tales of rivalry and achievements, while friends and colleagues can reveal how they are in their daily lives, as well as dishing the dirt on incidents that the groom might prefer to keep hidden! Old school chums can point to 'the way he has changed since he was in short

pants', or confirm how he was always destined to make his mark. Can you track down anything the groom might have written while at school, or a teacher's report on his progress?

◆ **Get background on the main guests, especially key relatives**.
Ask the groom who needs to be mentioned in your speech. There could be a mentor, a favourite aunt, a grandparent, who has played a significant role in the groom's early life, or someone who foresaw his potential and who will be particularly proud of him on his wedding day. However, don't have too many people prepared to say they knew the bride as a naked baby. She may not want repeated references to her bottom.

2. Being MC on the day

Unless a master of ceremonies or professional toast-master has been hired, you will be in charge and your duties will begin some time in advance, especially if there is to be a stag night. It will be up to you to organise it, to invite the gang, and to arrange the 'entertainment' to mark the end of the groom's single days. Then:

On the night before
◆ Make sure the groom gets to bed early and has an undisturbed night's sleep.

◆ Check the car you will be using, making sure it is clean inside and out, with enough petrol, oil and water.

◆ Tie a white ribbon on the bonnet, in case your car will be needed for formal duties the next day, then remove it and leave the ribbon in the glove compartment.

On the wedding day

◆ Rise early, dress smartly, and ensure that you have
  - money
  - credit cards
  - cheque book
  - keys
  - spectacles (if relevant)
  - any relevant paperwork relating to the wedding
  - mobile phone and important numbers, including the car hire people
  - guest list
  - your speech
  - the wedding ring(s).

◆ Help the groom to dress and look his best.

◆ Carry an **emergency kit**, including aspirin or paracetamol, antacid tablets, chewing gum or mints, tooth picks or floss, and deodorant.

◆ Make contact with the clergyman or registrar, the organist, the caterer, DJ or band leader, banqueting manager.

◆ Pay those who need paying. Get receipts.

◆ Check that the **ushers** are all properly dressed, with matching outfits. Anything or anyone that is out of sync will stand out and spoil the symmetry of the occasion.

◆ Ask who are to be the two **witnesses** and brief them to attend at the right place and at the right time. It is usual for the Best Man to be one of the witnesses.

◆ Make arrangements to collect **out of town guests** from the station, if necessary, ensuring that those on 'taxi' stand-by do not park where their cars are hemmed in.

◆ Brief the ushers or groomsmen on escorting guests to their places for the ceremony: bride's people on the left facing the front, groom's people on the right facing front.

◆ On greeting couples, the correct form is to introduce yourself to the male guest and shake hands, then let him introduce his partner. If he doesn't do so, don't press it. Just introduce yourself to her later.

◆ Pay special attention to **unaccompanied women**. These should be offered an arm and escorted to their places.

◆ Decorate the **getaway car**. Involve the ushers or groomsmen: collect together some empty cans, string, old shoes and shaving foam.

3. At the reception

◆ Be in charge.

◆ Gather together all the cards and goodwill messages.

◆ Get yourself a glass of wine but don't drink it until after your speech.

◆ Make sure everyone knows where they will be sitting.

◆ Check that the bride's father is OK about his speech.

◆ Check if anyone else has been asked to speak and agree the running order.

◆ Cross-check the stories they will be telling about the couple, to ensure that there is no duplication.

♦ Look after the bridesmaids – you are their spokesman.

♦ If there is a microphone for the speeches, check that it works and where it will be placed.

♦ When it's your turn to speak **read out the cards**.

♦ Refer to absent relatives and friends.

♦ Acknowledge that you are speaking on behalf of the bridesmaids or matron of honour.

♦ Tell the bride how pretty she looks.

♦ Give advice to the groom.

♦ Tell a story or two about him (embarrassing, revealing, but clean).

♦ Tell the bride how pretty she looks.

♦ Give advice to the bride.

♦ Tell the bride how pretty she looks.

♦ Propose a toast to the couple (unless the bride's father has already done so).

♦ Alternatively, propose a toast to absent friends.

Handling difficult situations

Because you are in charge, *difficult situations* will become your responsibility. Typically, these might be:

- hired wedding car doesn't turn up

- a drunken guest

- unsuitable music

- embarrassing, amorous behaviour

- getaway car won't start

- the wedding meal is ruined.

Hired wedding car not there

Quickly extract the white ribbon from your glove compartment and attach it to the bonnet, as you practised the night before, and present the car as the handy replacement. You'll be glad you cleaned it the night before!

Drunken guest

Some drunkenness is inevitable, and might even be amusing, but if someone starts behaving obnoxiously, it's time to activate **operation extraction**. Place some burly groomsmen near the outside phone (for example), then send someone to tell the drunken guest he's wanted on the phone. Follow him out and when he arrives at the phone, explain that he needs to go home. Then speak to anyone who came with him and ask if they would like to take him home. Alternatively, call a cab and see him safely away.

Unsuitable music

Although you previously interviewed or auditioned the DJ or band leader and received a play list, it may be that the music choice or volume level is spoiling the party. Call for a break and quietly talk to the chap about a revised programme. If you have followed my advice and not paid fully in advance, the ace up your sleeve is withholding payment. But don't flash this card too early, or the chap might take umbrage and walk out, leaving you without any music. You can sue, of course, but the party will still be ruined.

Amorous behaviour

Your duties do not include being moral watchdog, but if the bride's father disappears into the bushes with a bridesmaid, try to prevent his wife from following them. Above all, don't make a play, yourself, for anyone with a ring on the third finger of her left hand. Her partner might be in the room, and a punch on the nose can sometimes offend.

Getaway car

If theirs won't start, offer them yours.

Ruined meal

Order pizzas, not forgetting the vegetarians.

CHAPTER 4

Planning Your Speech

Well said; that was laid on with a trowel.
William Shakespeare: *As You Like It.*

You stand up and call for silence.

Your throat is dry but the sweat drips off your forehead and your shirt is clinging to your back. There's a slow pounding in your head and your stomach is lurching around. The brilliant opening line that you crafted so carefully has fled from your memory and you yearn for someone to call you away to take an urgent telephone call. In your hand is a bundle of papers which you are crushing with the tension that is gripping you and blurring your vision. You look down at them and realise they are the cards that everyone is expecting you to read out.

You start to speak, but all you can do is squeak. You open the first card and the rest slip from your hand, cascading to the floor. The room erupts in laughter and you twist around, looking for a bin into which you can throw up. And as you do so, you fall out of bed.

It has all been a terrible dream, a nightmare, and possibly a recurrent one.

It is actually a fairly common nightmare, and its cause is simple: *fear of public speaking*. It is well documented that one of the greatest fears of modern man is public speaking. For some reason, people who may be fluent and confident in conversation will freeze in fear when they have to stand in the spotlight and deliver a speech, even if the audience consists of friends and family. It's fear of what might happen, fear of not meeting the unspoken expectations of others, fear of failing. It can happen to anyone, even experienced speakers. It has happened to me – although I have probably won more speech contests than anyone in Britain.

A few years ago, my son decided on a change of career, and left to train as a commercial pilot. Just before his departure, my daughter arranged a surprise party for him. When he was delivered, unsuspecting, into the garden where his friends were all gathered, amid the welcoming uproar my daughter came up to me, full of smiles, and said, 'You'll make a speech, won't you Dad?' Her assumption was that, being a champion speaker, I could simply magic a speech out of my repertoire.

My throat went dry, the sweat dripped off my brow and my shirt was suddenly clinging to my back . . . but I think you know the routine.

The way to conquer the dread is to plan and prepare.

Make it memorable

Let's consider what is expected of a best man's speech,

then let's set down the kind of **preparation** you might undertake. Let me first dispel one common (and dreadful) misapprehension. Don't be fooled into thinking that because the best man's speech is brief and (relatively) informal it requires little or no preparation.

Abraham Lincoln's Gettysburg Address was brief. Delivered at the National Cemetery on 19th November 1863, it consisted of **265 words** and took between two and three minutes to deliver. Yet the man who had spoken at length before him said Lincoln had achieved more in his two minutes than he himself had managed in the previous two hours. Of the two, whose speech, would you say, made more of an impact or has endured to this day? We don't know how long Lincoln spent on crafting his 265 words, but we do remember his words:

> 'Four score and seven years ago our fathers brought forth upon this continent a new nation, conceived in liberty and dedicated to the proposition that all men are created equal. Now we are engaged in a great civil war, testing whether that nation, or any nation so conceived and so dedicated, can long endure. We are met on a great battlefield of that war. We have come to dedicate a portion of that field as a final resting-place of those who here gave their lives that that nation might live. It is altogether fitting and proper that we should do this. But in a larger sense we cannot dedicate, we cannot consecrate,

we cannot hallow this ground. The brave men, living and dead, who struggled here, have consecrated it far and above our power to add or detract.

The world will little note, nor long remember, what we say here, but it can never forget what they did here. It is for us, the living, rather to be dedicated here to the unfinished work they have thus far so nobly advanced. It is rather for us to be here dedicated to the great task remaining before us, that from these honoured dead we take increased devotion to that cause for which they here gave the last full measure of devotion; that we here highly resolve that the dead shall not have died in vain, that this nation, under God, shall have a new birth of freedom; and that government of the people, by the people, and for the people, shall not perish from the earth.'

When Lincoln said, *'The world will little note, nor long remember, what we say here,'* he was wrong. The world has never forgotten his words. The bride and groom, and the wedding guests, will probably never forget yours, so let's make your words worth remembering.

Expectations

Of all wedding speeches, the **best man's speech** is the one most looked forward to. You are expected to be funny, witty and revealing. You must be a showman, a stand-up comedian and straight man for the odd drunken heckler who fancies himself as the master of repartee. In short, you are expected to provide the channel for laughter.

Fortunately, you have three factors in your favour:

1. Everyone wants you to succeed.

2. Your audience has been well lubricated, and will laugh at anything even moderately funny.

3. You are the last speaker, and the audience has therefore been warmed up for you.

You have probably been acting as **master of ceremonies** or host, and are therefore already known to everyone there, and that might be a fourth factor in your favour.

You will be expected to reveal *why you were chosen as best man*, and tell a story or two about your relationship with the groom. People will want to hear about the groom's early years, and gasp at his (repeatable) indiscretions. They will want you to provide the prompt to laugh (kindly) at the groom, and his relatives will want to be mentioned or acknowledged by you.

They will also want you to read out any **cards and other messages** sent by those not able to be there. (Here's one from his brother: it says, *'Sorry I couldn't be there, but I* *wasn't invited.'*) All these expectations mean that you need to start early and do your research. Have a **notebook** clearly labelled '**Best Man's Speech**', and jot down anything that might be of help to you, any phrases, paragraphs, jokes, stories. Also have a large envelope with the same label. Into it you should drop any scraps of paper or old envelopes on which you may have scribbled ideas when you did not have your notebook handy.

Match the mood

It is very important to pitch your speech to suit the occasion and the audience. Get it wrong and everyone will shuffle their feet and squirm. Get it right and they will laugh and thank you for being such a jolly fellow. So it is important to start by asking the groom about the kind of guests he is expecting. Don't be satisfied with the labels he offers you ('There'll be the managing director of my wife's firm, a retired Admiral of the Fleet, three Members of Parliament and Lord Bloggs of Hadrian's Wall...') as that may create quite the wrong expectation in you. Ask him to tell you what kind of people they are, how old, why they are coming, what their interests are, and so on. You need to get a feel for the kind of mood the party might have, especially if you don't know the people. That will guide you in the kind of questions you should ask when you set about the next stage of your research.

Talk to the **groom's relatives**, especially close ones. Ask them what they remember of the groom as a child: what was he good at, how did he get on at school, was he competitive with his **siblings**, what did people say about him and his likely prospects? Think about your own childhood, and how **aunts and uncles** used to talk about you and where they thought you might end up. It happens in all families, and it's a good indication of how the groom appeared to others in his younger days. How has he changed since then, or has he actually turned out just the way people expected?

Once you have decided whether he changed or remained the same, ask for anecdotes to illustrate that. At the same time, find out the nature of the relationship between the source of the story and the groom. By that I mean, did they get on, were they close, or was the source a barely tolerated, infrequent visitor? You may be able to make something of the connection.

Next, talk to the groom's colleagues at work. How do they perceive him? Can they offer you stories of the odd faux pas?

- ◆ 'On his first day at work, he asked a chap in the corridor to post a letter for him. It turned out to be the MD.'

Or some amazing success?

◆ 'In his first month they gave him a sales target that no one had ever reached, but he didn't know that, so he just did what they told him to do and he not only reached the target but exceeded it by 20 per cent!'

When you talk to these people, *listen carefully for any hint of negative feedback*, and steer away from it. You are not researching his suitability for a job. Your purpose is to find positive and amusing things to tell about him, even if they include a bit of leg pulling.

Speak to the **parents** of both the bride and the groom. You are looking for the *'Ah!' factor*. Something to tug at the heartstrings. But leaven the sentimentality with embarrassing photographs, if you can persuade them to find some and lend them to you. You need something that can be blown up large and seen by the whole gathering when you produce it during your speech. So go for quality rather than quantity.

Just remember, if you are lent something of sentimental value, copy it if possible and return the original right away. It causes great distress and lingering resentment if such items (even single photographs) are not returned.

Talk to the groom's siblings and/or cousins – anyone who grew up with the groom and perhaps went to the same school. Here you are looking for unalloyed embarrassment. Usually brothers will be only too glad to dish the dirt about some unfortunate episode or two in the distant past, and perhaps even come up with a photograph the groom would rather forget (like Tony Blair in flares).

It's better to do too much research than not enough. You may not use all the material in your speech, but you will certainly benefit from the insights you will gain from your conversations. Who knows, it might even cause you to regard the groom with greater awe!

In the next two chapters we'll see how you can arrange the material and construct a speech that is easy to remember and a pleasure to deliver.

CHAPTER 5

Preparation

Making sure you are ready for the challenge

Preparing the best man's speech is no different from preparing any other speech. The same disciplines apply. Like any other speech:

◆ it is a piece of spoken communication

◆ through which one person (you) connects with an audience and

◆ seeks to bring about a change in their state of mind.

That's a pompous way of saying you'll be trying to make them feel good. You'll also be trying to make yourself *feel* good, *look* good, *sound* good.

Above all, you'll be trying to *avoid any of the negative scenarios* that have been filling you with dread ever since you agreed to be best man. In this chapter and the next one I shall take you slowly **through each step of preparing and writing a speech**. Although we shall be working on this specific speech, the lessons will be useful to you on every other occasion when you have to stand on your hind legs and address an audience.

If you are already an experienced speaker or presenter, you may want to skip to the next chapter. Most people, however, will find it useful to follow the points of preparation in this chapter, even if it does seem simplistic. I'll give you **a step-by-step procedure** that will take away the anxiety of preparation and keep you on track. It's a no-brainer. Follow it and you'll end up with a speech that you'll be pleased to deliver.

The reasoning behind the sequence in these two chapters is that **it takes a great deal of nervous energy** to compose a speech, however brief. It's hard to know how much research to do and when to stop. It's difficult to decide how to shape all the ideas you may gather in your research. And it's tough to apply all the necessary disciplines to preparing the speech. I'll try to make it easy for you.

The disciplines I have in mind are:

◆ content
◆ structure or sequence
◆ language
◆ use of humour, and
◆ duties.

What you already know

Let's start by reminding you of what you already know, and what it means for your speech.

◆ You know that the best man concept *originated in the days when brides were abducted,* and her friends and family had to be fought off. Your stance must therefore be protective of the groom, even though you may pull his leg and even embarrass him a bit.

◆ You know that you were selected because of *your special relationship* with the groom, and that therefore you can provide some insights and perhaps even divulge a secret or two.

◆ You know that you are *expected to be amusing,* and that you need to have a joke or two, but not the stale stuff that everyone has heard before.

◆ You know that you may have had to act as *master of ceremonies,* and that therefore you will have already made some impression on the audience.

◆ You know that you have to collect together the *cards and messages* from absent family and friends, so you must plan how and when to read them out.

◆ You know that your speech will be in *response to a toast to the bridesmaids or matron of honour,* and that you must therefore be gallant and gracious.

◆ You know that *yours is a pivotal role* in the day's proceedings, and you should be masterful and 'in charge'.

◆ You know that this is a wonderful *opportunity to make a big impression*, which could benefit you in your working life and may even lead to a speaking career. Many professional speakers started by making an unexpectedly impressive best man speech.

◆ You know what the groom's family and friends think of him, and what they want the world to know about him. You have privileged information about the day's key player, and you can use it to benefit him, yourself and the assembled company.

10 Key Points

You know all those things. That puts you in a very powerful position. It means you know what to say and you know that you will be well received because the wedding guests will see you as the one who knows what to do and say. So let's draw up a (flexible) checklist of the **10 key points** you should consider including in your stand-up slot. Here they are in no particular order. And don't worry, when you've read through them I'll show you how to arrange them in sequence, and the script will follow easily from that.

1. Your first duty is to **thank the groom** for the kind things he has said about the bridesmaids or maid of honour, as you are responding on their behalf.

2. Thank him also **for any gifts** he may have given to the other helpers: bridesmaids, ushers, page boys, and anyone else.

3. **Read the cards**, telegrams, mobile phone text messages and smoke signals sent in by those who could not attend the wedding in person.

4. Reveal some of the **heartstopping moments** leading up to the big day, including misunderstandings, wrong deliveries, amusing moments and near misses.

5. Select a couple of **revealing anecdotes** from your early relationship with the groom.

6. Put in some mildly **embarrassing revelations** about the groom's younger life – at school, at work, when he joined the Young Conservatives, when he switched to the Lib Dems, when he disgraced himself at some formal function . . . that kind of thing. Just remember not to be hurtful. It's his day and he needs to be helped to feel good about it all. Pull his leg but don't tear it off.

7. **Use props** to highlight your main embarrassing revelation(s). This could be photographic evidence of his stag night, Blair in Flares, or a pic of him going purple in the face as he strained into his nappy at a tender age.

8. **Say nice things about the bride**. Tell her how lovely she looks. Speak to both of them directly, part of the time, but don't address the whole speech to them.

9. Add a **touch of sincerity** near the end. Talk about the good mate he has been, about how he behaved differently 'with this one', and how she came to replace his former bachelor pursuits.

10. Conclude with a **toast**. If the bride's father hasn't already done so, toast the bride and groom. Otherwise toast absent friends.

Sequence

Once you have set down all the material you need to include, it's relatively easy to arrange it in the order you should follow. Do you need to follow a sequence? Of course you do. Your listeners do not know what you have planned on saying, nor will they readily follow your drift unless you make it easy for them to see how each point follows from the previous one and leads on to the next. If you drift from one unconnected thought to another, your listeners' minds will also drift, and they'll stop listening to you.

Even if your mother and both your friends try hard to be supportive and laugh at all your jokes, you'll soon notice that the rest of the room is simply waiting for your lips to stop moving, so they can get on with the dancing.

So the next chapter is devoted to organizing your material and drafting that all-important speech.

CHAPTER 6

Writing the Speech in Eight Steps

Now here's how to make it easy to arrive at the first draft.

Step 1: 10 Key Points

Get 10 sheets of paper, one for each of the 10 key points, and label (but do not number) them at the top like this:

1. Responding for bridesmaids/maid of honour

2. Thanks for gifts

3. Cards and messages

4. Background mishaps

5. Me and the groom

6. Embarrassing stuff

7. Props to use

8. Talking to the bride

9. Sincere stuff

10. Concluding toast

Step 2: Brainstorm

Fill in the details. On each page write ideas and thoughts as bullet points, and add to them as the days pass. Write on both sides of the paper if you need to, and keep each point brief. At this stage all you are doing is an extended brainstorm, so there is no need to write complete sentences unless there is a particular turn of phrase that appeals to you and you don't want to risk forgetting it. Add any relevant quotations to the appropriate page. And don't eliminate anything. Even stray ideas can lead to better ones.

They could look like this:

Responding for bridesmaids

◆ Address vicar, bride and groom, ladies and gentlemen.

◆ Thanks for kind words.

◆ Speaking on their behalf.

◆ Origin of custom.

◆ Compliment them.

Background mishaps

◆ Disco not booked. DJ ill, did not inform us until we checked a week ago.

◆ Groom booked for Amsterdam conference starting yesterday.

◆ Vicar said we had to be quick, as he was double-booked.

◆ Invitations stated wrong starting time.

When you've put down all you can think of, it's time to move to the next stage:

Step 3: Planning the Sequence

Based on the ideas on each page, place the 10 pages in the order in which you think you should cover them in your speech. Then number the pages in that order. They will probably come out like this:

1. Responding for bridesmaids/maid of honour

2. Thanks for gifts

3. Talking to the bride

4. Background mishaps

5. Me and the groom

6. Embarrassing stuff

7. Props to use

8. Sincere stuff

9. Cards and messages

10. Concluding toast

Now it's time for the next stage:

Step 4: editing

Run down the list of items on each page and delete anything that doesn't fit. Then, on a fresh sheet of paper, write all the points you've decided to keep in. That will be the basis for your speech. There are just a couple of steps left, and then it will be time to talk about delivery – how you put across the speech and make a lasting impression.

Step 5: First Draft

You can do this in one of two ways: if you are reasonably good at writing, write out a complete script, based on the sequence of points you have just put on paper; alternatively, talk about them into a tape recorder, and transcribe that onto paper.

Step 6: Rewrite

Tidy up your **first draft**, so that the language you use is conversational. Remember that the text that is written to be said is different from the text that is written to be read. Change any words or phrases that cause you to stumble (when you've had even one drink, under stress, you'll stumble even more). Don't try to write it like an article or an essay.

Here's the opening sentence from a newspaper article. Does it read like something you'd say to a pal in the pub?

Ancestor worship is the most ancient and universal of cultural beliefs, embedded in secular tradition as well as religion, a ritual of self-validation as ancient as time.

Wouldn't it be better to say something like this:

Many groups of people throughout history have worshipped their ancestors. Ordinary people as well as priests and monks. It has been a way of saying, 'This is who I am'.

Two more steps.

Step 7: Write a Hook

That's an opening that catches the attention of your audience. It should be something dramatic, something unexpected, or a story. You do need to catch the attention of your listeners right from the start. A hook creates a mental picture in the minds of your listeners. They can then follow your narrative as though they were watching a video. Avoid using words that are only about abstract concepts or general terms. For example, which of these two sentences makes a picture in *your* mind?

A. I remember one December when I went to the High Street and was very impressed by the way the town was decorated for Christmas.

or

B. I drove to the High Street on a crisp December morning, and my jaw dropped at the fantastic sight of multi-coloured lights and greenery hanging from every lamp post.

Here's an example of a hook:

I was sitting alone in my bachelor pad, one night last May, doing what a bachelor does when he's alone, when the doorbell rang. I wasn't expecting anyone, so I ignored it. *Ding dong! Ding dong! Ding dong!* Whoever it was had decided to lean on the bell until I answered it, so finally I went and threw open the door, and there was Bill (the groom), all dishevelled with tie askew and hair all over the place, and that soppy, lopsided grin on his face. I could tell he'd been drinking. The bottle of champagne in his right hand was a dead giveaway. He burped, shot his arms in the air and shouted, 'I'm getting married! And I want you to be my best man!' I was too startled to refuse, and that's how I came to be standing here today, quivering like a jelly and wishing I hadn't been home that night.

Can you picture the scene? Do you get a feeling for the mood of the moment?

Step 8: Speaker's Notes

These consist of a summary of your text as headings and

bullet points on 5 x 3 cards. Even if you decide to memorise the complete script by heart, do not use the full script on the actual day, or you will be tempted to read them out, and that will lose your audience.

Here's an example of speaker's notes:

OPENING

◆ Address vicar/bride and groom/ladies and gentlemen

◆ Response on behalf of bridesmaids: compliment/ origin

◆ **Hook**: How I got the job

◆ How feeling: quivering like jelly

◆ Outline/map

Your speech might look something like this:

Reverend McCarthy, Bill and Jane, ladies and gentlemen.

It falls to me to respond on behalf of the bridesmaids, and I'm honoured that I have the opportunity to speak for two ladies as lovely as Mary and Christine. I suppose the custom dates back to the time when the best man was the leader of the gang that aided the groom in kidnapping his bride. These days the tongue is sharper than the sword, so the cut and thrust of my duties as best man are only verbal.

In a way, however, I might have been more proficient with a sword than with words. Let me tell you how I came to be best man today, and share with you some of the anxious moments we have encountered along the way. I have a collection of cards and other messages here, but I'll read them out at the end.

I was sitting alone in my bachelor pad, one night last May, doing what a bachelor does when he's alone, when the doorbell rang. I wasn't expecting anyone, so I ignored it. *Ding dong! Ding dong! Ding dong!* Whoever it was had decided to lean on the bell until I answered it, so finally I went and threw open the door, and there was Bill (the groom), all dishevelled with tie askew and hair all over the place, and that soppy, lopsided grin on his face. I could tell he'd been drinking. The bottle of champagne in his right hand was a dead giveaway. He burped, shot his arms in the air and shouted, 'I'm getting married! And I want you to be my best man!' I was too startled to refuse, and that's how I came to be standing here today, quivering like a jelly and wishing I hadn't been home that night.

It all seems to have come together at last, but it was touch and go, once or twice. Only one week ago I rang the disco DJ to confirm arrangements, only to discover that he'd been ill for some time and hadn't let us know. But that wasn't the worst of it.

No one told his office manager Bill was getting married, and he was booked to go on a computer conference in Amsterdam, starting yesterday. It was only a casual remark in the office that brought the clash of dates to light, and a replacement had to be found in a hurry. So Bill went to Amsterdam, and his replacement has just married Jane!

No, no, I was just kidding. This is the real Bill, in the flesh. Accept no cheap imitations. This is the one and only, unique and irreplaceable Bill Bradley, hero of the Somerset Close False Fire Alarm. Let me tell you the story...

Bill was in his mid-teens when he spent a summer holiday in a rented cottage in Somerset. One day his mother went out to the shops, leaving Bill to get his own lunch. When she returned, she found him asleep in front of the telly, with smoke billowing from the kitchen and the smoke alarm shrieking. She shook him awake, and he quickly realised that the house was on fire.

Being a man of action, he grabbed the phone, dialled 999, shouted 'Fire!' and dashed out of the house with his Mum. Five minutes later the fire brigade arrived, along with everyone else in the whole street. They rushed into the house with their hoses and emerged soon afterwards with some burnt bits of potato.

Bill had put a potato into the microwave, which he had never used before, set it for half an hour, then sat in front of the telly and forgotten all about it. The result was a huge amount of smoke, but no fire.

That incident propelled Bill into the world of technical skill and made him the computer wizard that he is today.

Let me now show you some evidence of his progression from kitchen nerd to computer king. (Produce set of photographs and touch on each one briefly.)

Jane, I must say you are looking fantastic today. Bill's a very lucky chap. But in a way, you are lucky too, because Bill is also a super bloke and a great friend. His incompetence in some ways may have made him a legend in his own lunchtime, but he is always excellent company and someone who never lets you down. I wish you both a long and happy life together.

(The father of the bride usually toasts the couple, but if you are asked to do so, just continue by saying:)

Well, ladies and gentlemen, I know you would want to join me in wishing the new Mr and Mrs Bradley a long and happy married life, so please stand and join me in a toast to Bill and Jane. The toast is:

Bill and Jane.

Now it's time to rehearse.

CHAPTER 7

Things to Avoid

There are some things the best man should not do and quite a few things he should not say.

Past relationships

The golden rule is to avoid mentioning any previous girlfriend. At all. The most you should venture is something general like, 'I contacted all his past girlfriends' or even 'I looked out of the window and there was a mile-long queue of disappointed women'. But do not mention any of them by name. This is the bride's day and it should not be tainted by the thought of any other woman. If he has a past, she knows whatever he wants her to know, or whatever she chooses to know, and you should respect that.

Punctuality

As best man, you are in charge of the day's arrangements, and you must not be late at any stage of the proceedings. Even if you have to sleep in the vestry with the wedding ring hung on a string around your neck, you must be there early.

What's more, you have got to make sure the groom is ready and on time too. The bride will not enter the church until the groom is there.

Jilting

If the unthinkable happens and the groom has cold feet at the last moment, **don't allow him to bolt!** The groom is entitled to change his mind at the last moment, but he is not entitled to humiliate the bride by not turning up. It is your duty to ensure that he does turn up at the church or register office, even if it is only to apologise and call off the wedding. But do not collude in any cowardly behaviour.

Humiliation

Everyone has some sort of skeleton in the closet. As best man you know something either because you were present or because you uncovered it in your researches. Don't yield to the temptation to get a cheap laugh by revealing the secret. You may think it's funny, but it may be deeply embarrassing (and even humiliating) for the groom, and something he's been trying to forget.

You could totally ruin his day (and his reputation) by being careless. The golden rule is: if in doubt, leave it out, but in this case, be in no doubt that you must leave it out.

Pomposity

Don't be pompous. For example, you may know that certain customs or traditions have not been observed in that day's proceedings. Don't be tempted to show off what you know.

Language

One young man I knew when we were both in our 20s, used to adopt a style of speaking that his great-grandfather might have used, whenever he rose to make a speech. He used long words that he barely understood and could hardly pronounce. He thought he was being impressive, but actually people used to laugh at him. Use the language of everyday speech. Speak as though you were talking to your mates in the pub. And when you propose your toast, there is no need to say, 'Please be upstanding'. It's good enough to say, 'Please rise' or even 'Please stand'.

Also, do avoid saying 'a bumper toast'. The word 'bumper', when used as a noun, means a drinking vessel filled to the brim or, in Australia, a cigarette butt, and therefore something useless. As an adjective it means 'abundant'. As a verb, it means to drink a toast to someone, as in 'bumper the groom'. Yet, the phrase, 'drink a bumper toast to ___' has become commonplace, and marks its user as someone who is likely also to say, 'between you and I'.

Accent

Putting on a falsely posh accent is the ultimate in pompous behaviour. Very few people do it these days, thank goodness, but it does still happen. Don't let it happen to you. Be yourself. You were asked to be best man because of who you are, so there's no need to try to pretend you are someone else.

Off-colour jokes and swearing

Risqué jokes are risky. Where do you draw the line? You can be as bawdy as you like at the stag party, but why risk offending anyone at the wedding reception? My own view is that a *double entendre* may be just about acceptable if it is clever, but never forget that there may be children present as well as aged relatives whose standards may be different from your own. The same caution applies to strong language. In this case do **not** talk as you would to your mates in the pub!

Tell the truth

Under no circumstances should you tell a lie or even 'shade' the truth for effect. People will take literally what you say. I once knew a blind chap whose regular form of exercise was to go tandem cycling with a female friend. His wife accepted that the relationship was entirely proper. In a speech I was giving, I told a tandem-riding joke about him and his female companion. It was at a sports club dinner, and everyone knew the story was only a joke (I assumed), but he protested aloud as soon as I started the joke. Quite rightly, he didn't want to be accused of any impropriety, even in jest.

Other forms of untruths can be even more harmful, so it's best to stick closely to the truth in everything you say.

Unkind references

Do not mock anyone in your speech. Say nothing that can offend. Do not refer unkindly to someone else's looks, behaviour or disabilities. It's easy to make a mistake: I was walking down the High Street with a friend one day, when a man with a white stick asked us where the Halifax Building Society was. I said: 'You've passed it. Come on, we'll walk there with you.' Along the way, I decided to tell him where we were, to help him get his bearings for the future, so I said, 'Now we are walking past Woolworth's.' At this, and without thinking, my friend said, 'That doesn't mean anything to him, he's as blind as a bat.' Imagine making a gaffe like that in your speech. Worse still, imagine *deliberately* saying something like that...

Behaviour

◆ Don't get drunk.

◆ *Don't flirt* with the bridesmaids or matron of honour or any of the invited relatives – at all, if you're married. And if you're single, don't do it at the expense of your duties as best man.

- *Never* make a pass at the bride. Not even if she encourages you.

- Don't spend all your time talking to the groom's family, just because you know them, ignoring the bride's family. Balance your attentions. Remember, you will be seen as an important person on the day, and guests will be pleased to have a few words with you during the reception, so circulate.

- If anything upsets or offends you, *do not sulk.* Your first obligation is to the groom and his new bride, so grin and bear it, and remain enthusiastic.

- *Don't get drunk.*

- *Do not quarrel with the groom.* He may be stressed and get stroppy at times. It's only natural, and he needs someone who will put up with it and be as steady as the Rock of Gibraltar. That's why he asked you to be his best man in the first place.

- If anyone comes to you with a problem, whether it's about the food or the state of the toilets, do not say, 'It's nothing to do with me.' *Sort it out.* You may not be the host, but you are seen to be in charge.

- Don't disregard the *bride's parents.* Usually it is they who have paid for the party, so they are, in effect, *your hosts*. Act as though the reception is being held in their home.

◆ Don't try to do it all yourself. *Delegate* some tasks to the ushers.

◆ **Don't get drunk**.

◆ *Don't allow the groom to get drunk*. Not at the stag party and not at the wedding reception. It's not worth the fallout.

CHAPTER 8

The Big Day

This chapter is a sort of reminder of the things you should be doing or thinking about on the big day. Elsewhere in the book you have detailed guidance on all the essentials, but the night before, and on the day itself, you may want a brief summary. If, during your preparations in the weeks before the wedding, you think of something that you don't want to forget, write it down in this chapter.

Here's where you will find:

– how to prepare yourself in your mind

– 20 top tips

– more good advice.

The night before

◆ Have your clothing set out.

◆ Call the groom and ensure he sets out his clothing.

◆ Check that you have the ring(s).

◆ Check the car.

◆ Check that you have the ring(s).

◆ Check that you have the Order of Service sheets.

◆ Check that you have the ring(s).

The Big Day dawns

1. Listen to the tape of your speech while you are getting dressed.

2. Call the groom and make sure he's all right.

3. Be on time.

4. Have your speech ready with at least two copies.

5. Call the ushers.

6. Call the car hire company.

7. Make sure you have the wedding ring(s) in your ticket pocket.

8. Check that you have:
   - cash
   - cheque book
   - credit cards
   - copy of speech (x 2)
   - mobile phone
   - essential numbers, including florist, caterer, reception hall, car hire company, vicar, bride's father

◆ the honeymoon pack.

9. Place groom at the front of the church or register office, then give ushers final briefing:
   ◆ buttonholes

   ◆ order of service

   ◆ bride's side

   ◆ groom's side

   ◆ unaccompanied ladies

   ◆ collecting guests from station

   ◆ confetti: obey the wishes of the clergyman or the register official.

10. Assist photographer in grouping the wedding party.

11. Pay the clergyman and anyone else who needs paying that day.

12. Drink no alcohol before your speech: stay 'on duty' until the bride and groom have left.

13. Agree the order of speaking.

14. Ensure that the tables are cleared before speeches start.

15. Three point preparation.

16. Mentally rehearse your opening paragraph.

17. Remember, everyone wants you to succeed.

18. Use your notes and take your time.

19. End with a toast.

20. Decorate the getaway car.

More good advice

◆ If it is a formal wedding, get the ushers and bridesmaids to help you set up a **receiving line**, with the bride and groom welcoming every guest in turn.

◆ **Speeches** start as soon as coffee has been served at the end of the meal.

◆ **Identify yourself** and explain your relationship with the groom. Not everyone can be expected to know who you are.

◆ Stand up, speak up, shut up.

◆ Use your notes.

◆ **Thank the hosts** (bride's parents or the bride and groom) for inviting everyone to share the big occasion.

◆ **Thank the groom** for inviting you to be best man.

◆ **Thank all who helped** with the day's arrangements.

◆ **Flatter the bride.** She's all dressed up and feeling great, so tell her how wonderful she looks.

◆ Tell an **amusing story** or two about the groom. Make 'em laugh if you can.

◆ If you have a **joke** or two that you can deliver well, *make it relevant* to the occasion. Use links such as, 'Something (the groom) said to me on our way here this morning reminded me of the time, ten years ago, when...'

◆ Read out the **cards and other messages** from those who are not there.

◆ End with an **uplifting message** of hope for the future happiness of the couple, and **propose a toast** to:
  – **the bride and groom** or (if already done by bride's father)
  – **absent friends and family.**

◆ Introduce the **bride's speech**, if she has indicated that she would like to say a few words. It may not be traditional, but it's her day, so why not?

◆ Get the ushers to help you decorate the **getaway car** with shaving cream, tin cans and/or old shoes, string, white ribbon and balloons.

◆ Hand the couple their **honeymoon pack**, including passports and tickets, and anything else related to the honeymoon.

◆ Make sure that all the **wedding gifts** are delivered safely to the bride's home or that of her parents.

Best Man's Plan

The best man is *not* responsible for arranging a wedding. He *is* responsible, though, for making the big day run smoothly. He's the one who sees the pieces are picked up if the waiter drops the cake. It's his job to ensure that details, disasters, or drunks do not mar the day for the bride and groom and their families.

This is not as difficult as it sounds. Everybody present will want the day to be a big success. So, too, will the hotelier who is hoping for other bookings. So be a good manager and delegate. The groom's father might collect and return the suits, the bride's brother look after lifts.

It must be remembered too that weddings are happy occasions. People are out to have a day's fun and enjoyment. Nobody is going to be too upset if everything isn't done exactly according to the etiquette books. In fact many people find all the etiquette confusing and unnecessary. That sometimes includes the groom and the best man!

Basically good manners and common sense are far more important than written rules. Do remember that being asked to be best man is an honour as well as a responsibility. So if you want to relax and enjoy the day the secret is to be like the Boy Scouts and 'Be Prepared'.

PS If you've brought mix and match speeches you'll need a roll of Sellotape and scissors to cut and paste selected paragraphs.

Summary of Duties

Read this plan first. You can tick off your duties as they are done.

◆ Be helpful to the groom and look after the guests. Get the groom and the rings to the altar on time.

◆ Check that the ushers know their duties and pay the appropriate fees on behalf of the groom. See everyone has transport.

◆ Act as MC at the table and give a speech in reply to the groom's toast to the bridesmaids.

◆ Get the groom off on his honeymoon and his guests and his gifts safely home.

There are no rules about it but a good best man will have an **emergency kit**. These might include a few aspirin, a safety pin, a sticking plaster and, in some climates, an umbrella. He might also have, for visitors, a few copies of a map showing the journey from church/civil ceremony to hotel. A pen and notebook may come in useful too.

Before the wedding

◆ **Be available** to help the bride and groom with forward planning for the wedding. This could mean anything from helping them choose a nice hotel for the reception to offering to collect visiting guests at the airport. They may be very well organised themselves of course. Basically though it means being there for them if, and when, necessary.

◆ **Book your suit** for the wedding about eight weeks in advance and arrange to collect it before the wedding. It might be nice if you also arranged to collect the groom's suit.

◆ **Organise the stag night.** If a lot of old friends are coming it may be better to have it in a private room in a hotel or pub. Remember to ensure that taxis or lifts are organised for those who want to drink. Remember too that practical jokes can get out of hand. So don't let anyone do anything outrageous. It's your job to see the groom gets married not to have the bride call it off before they even get to the church!

◆ **Prepare a transport list.** Many people prefer not to drive to weddings because they know they will be drinking. There will probably be no trouble organising lifts, as there are usually lots of cars. Every family, though, has its elderly relatives who need to be collected. It's thoughtful to think of their needs and to assure them that they will be collected.

◆ **Attend the rehearsal** if there is one. Note who is giving readings or saying prayers and nominate a replacement just in case someone doesn't turn up. That way you'll avoid uncomfortable pauses in the ceremony.

◆ **Be available** to do any last minute chores for the groom in the busy few days before the wedding itself.

Select your speech and stick it on cue cards. Then cut and paste the following introductions on cue cards too for use at the wedding meal. Remember that if someone on the list is not going to speak, or there is no grace, you will have to remove the relevant cue card(s). At many weddings you may only need two or three cue cards altogether.

1st cue card

Entrance of bride and groom.

'Ladies and gentlemen, please rise for the bride and groom.'

Cue card 2

Invitation to say grace.

'I shall now ask (title of clergyman) to say grace.'

Cue card 2a. (If no clergyman is present)

Best man's invitation to say grace.

'Ladies and gentlemen, please rise now to say grace.

Lord, thank you for this wedding meal
And those who've come to share
The bounty of your love, Lord,
Please keep us in your care.'

Cue card 3

Cutting the cake.

'Ladies and gentlemen, the bride and groom will now cut the cake.'

Cue card 4

Speech of the father of the bride.

'I now have pleasure in inviting the father of the bride

(or his representative) to give the speech he's been rehearsing since his daughter became engaged.'

Cue card 4a (if applicable)
Bride's speech.

'We now have an unexpected pleasure perhaps, a speech from the bride herself.'

Cue card 4b (if applicable)
Bridesmaid's speech.

'Not to be outdone by all the men our beautiful bridesmaid would like to say a few words on this special occasion.'

Cue card 5
Speech of the father of the groom (or his representative).

'And now, the moment you have all been waiting for, the man without whom there would be no wedding at all. Ladies and gentlemen, I give you the father of the groom.'

Cue card 6
Speech of the groom.

'The next speaker is the man of the moment himself. I now have great pleasure in calling on the groom to give us his thoughts on the day.'

Final cue card
The best man's speech.

'Now when everything seems to be said already I am supposed to find something wise and witty to add.'

(Place the cue cards containing your selected speech here.)

Extra cue card (if applicable)
Cards of congratulations.

'I would now like to read you some of the messages which have been sent to Mary and John today.'

Sometimes the bride and groom wish the meal to end with a toast to absent friends. Check this beforehand.

Morning of Wedding

◆ Have you organised your own transport needs today? Remember you will be going to the church or register office with the groom but you will be leaving without him. Will you need to have transport at the hotel so that you can run the bride and groom to the airport?

◆ Most hotels supply changing rooms for the bride and groom. Leave the groom's suitcases and going away clothes locked away there on the morning of the wedding.

◆ Collect the ring(s) and take any documents pertaining to the honeymoon such as tickets or passports or money.

◆ Collect the envelopes for church dues.

◆ Help the groom dress up and calm down. Does he need silver coins representing all his worldly goods?

◆ Have you got your cue cards in your pocket? Are they in the right order?

Wedding Day in Church

◆ Take the groom to church. Sometimes the groom goes to the church in the car, which will then return to the bride's home to collect her. Otherwise make sure you are both in plenty of time.

◆ Check that the church leaflets are available.

◆ Ensure that the groom, groomsmen, ushers and two fathers have buttonholes. Traditionally they are white except for the ushers, who wear red.

◆ Explain to the ushers that it is their responsibility to distribute the leaflets and usher ladies to their seats (on their right arms).

◆ Groom's guests are on right side of the church, bride's on the left. Mutual guests should balance the sides if numbers are uneven.

◆ The groom's mother should be escorted to the seat at the front directly behind her son.

◆ The bride's mother should be on the bride's side. She should only take her place just before the bride enters with her father.

◆ Once the bridesmaids arrive, the groom, best man and groomsmen take their places on the front seats at the right of the altar.

◆ The best man stands to the right of the groom.

◆ During the ceremony the best man produces the ring/s and witnesses the ceremony. Afterwards he walks with the chief bridesmaid to the registry where he witnesses the signing of the register. He then gives the sacristan or clerk the envelopes containing dues for the parish, the sacristan, the altar boys and, if necessary, the organist.

◆ The best man walks out of the church in the bridal procession escorting the chief bridesmaid. It is his duty to see that everyone has a lift to the hotel or wherever the reception is being held.

Wedding Day in Hotel/Club

♦ The best man arrives to join the reception line. In practice this is often a very relaxed and informal greeting of guests.

♦ The best man ensures that guests are ushered into the dining room and also that they all know where they are seated. It's nice if people can be directed to their tables quickly, particularly the elderly. It's worth considering that they may be hard of hearing and like to be near the top table. It's something to mention to the bride and groom, as they may not have thought of it.

♦ The best man ensures the safety of any gifts, which are brought for the bride and groom. These should be safely locked away in one of their changing rooms or, if necessary, in the hotel safe.

Wedding Meal

Now is the time to use those cue cards you have in your pocket.

The best man brings the meal to a close by asking the guests to allow staff to clear up for the dancing. Later on he or the bandleader ask the bridal couple to lead the dancing.

Wrapping up

When they are leaving the best man sees that the groom has his luggage, his travel tickets and his money. He then either leaves him at the destination of his choice or arranges for it to be done. Otherwise he shows where he has cleverly hidden the honeymoon car so that guests are unable to write wedding slogans on it.

When the happy couple has left, the best man arranges for the gifts to be brought somewhere for safety and collects the dress suits to bring them (if necessary) back to the suit hire company the following working day. Hopefully he then has time to enjoy the party before he finally ensures that everyone has a lift home.

The party's over

Your final official duty is to ensure the suits are returned to the dress hire company the following day. As a good friend, though, the groom may have asked you to keep on eye on his new home or to collect him at the airport after the honeymoon.

Hopefully the groom will bring you home the order of merit badge. You deserve it! Failing that, the least the bride may do is to make a match for you with one of her beautiful friends!

PS If one wedding really does lead to another you'll probably be asked to be best man again. You are, after all, an expert now!

Extra

I have included this checklist to keep in your pocket with the other cue cards. So cut it and place it on another cue card. You may find it gives you useful reminders on the big day.

Checklist

☐ Arrange your own transport for later.

☐ Are the cases in the changing rooms?

☐ Have you rings and fees (in envelopes) for church or register office fees?

☐ Check order of service leaflets are available.

☐ Have you the buttonholes?

☐ Explain duties to ushers.

☐ Groom's guests right side. Bride's guests left.

☐ Stand next to the groom at the front row.

☐ Witness ceremony/produce ring(s).

☐ Pay fees.

☐ Escort chief bridesmaid from church.

☐ See to lifts and act as MC.

☐ Check groom has travel documents and money.

☐ Take back suits the following day (if applicable).

☐ Well done!

CHAPTER 9

Delivery

Putting it across

After you have sweated blood to produce a speech that would make your mother proud, the temptation is to hide behind the script and read out those jewelled phrases. It would spare you the agony of looking the audience in the eye or of trying to remember your witty lines.

One word of advice: don't.

No matter how nervous or inexpert you may think you are, and however convinced you are that your face will explode or that the earth will open up and swallow you whole, it will not be as bad as you imagine, once you get started. Unless you read the script. Because when you have finished you will realise that there were no dragons there, and you will wish you had delivered your speech from the heart (and probably by heart, too) instead of from the page. The wedding guests will be patient and tolerant (they usually are), but they, too, will wish you had done a better job.

So let's consider how you can do the best job of delivering your lines, whether you learn your speech by heart or simply rely on speaker's notes. The first thing to bear in mind is that a speech is much more than the words you write. If the words alone were enough, you might just as well print out a batch of copies and hand them around.

Obviously that would not have the same effect, nor would it be appreciated as much as when you stand and deliver. That's because you add a vital dimension to the process. It's because the stories you tell and the way you speak about the bride and groom are personal to you, and they help the guests to understand something more about the newlyweds – something they did not know before, something that matters to them because they care about the couple. But that's not all. They want to see and hear from you, and they will admire a fine performance by you.

Let's consider how to put across the speech you have so carefully researched and crafted. And by the way, you do need to have spent time on preparation before reading this chapter. There's little point in rehearsing a speech that is likely to fail because of insufficient preparation, just as there is no point in reinforcing bad habits.

In this chapter we'll concentrate on your delivery, and on developing the techniques that will enable you to make a good impression. Many a business person contacts me shortly before a major speech or presentation and asks for a one-day 'quick fix'. This chapter contains many of the points I cover with them, and you have the advantage of having longer than a single day to practise them, and to refer back to these pages whenever you need to.

Correct breathing helps you sound better

Take a deep breath, then start counting aloud, at about one-second intervals, and see how far you get. Anything over 30 is good, but don't be surprised if you conk out before that.

Now stand up. Push your chair back and give yourself some space. Make sure you cannot be seen by anyone who might make you feel inhibited. I'm going to take you through a simple breathing exercise that will expand your lungs' capacity, especially if you practise it regularly, and clear your head as well.

- ◆ Take a deep breath.

- ◆ Hold it for the count of two.

- ◆ Then breathe out completely.

- ◆ When you think you have breathed out all the air from your lungs, try to blow out six candles, to really empty your lungs.

Then breathe in again, as deeply as you can. Once again, hold it for the count of two, breathe right out, and blow out six more candles.

Do that for the third time, then relax. If your head is feeling light, it's a good sign, and means your brain is now getting more oxygen than it was getting previously. Stay standing and wait for your head to feel normal again. Still standing, take a deep breath, and start counting again at the same pace as before. Did you get further this time? Do that exercise regularly, and see how you improve.

What's more, if you do that just before you stand to make your speech, you are less likely to forget your lines.

Now let's turn to your performance when you stand to deliver your speech.

Consider the scene. There was the wedding ceremony itself, with its traditions and its touch of formality. Family members who see one another only at weddings and funerals exchanged oohs and aahs, admired each others' hats and commented on how they might have changed since they last met. The organised chaos in front of the photographer's camera was the occasion for a wag or two to loose off the jokes they'd been rehearsing all week, and then they girded their loins for the 'wedding meal', fortified by gin and tonic or lager, and cheeks aching from the forced smiles of such occasions.

Now the meal is over, and the staff have cleared away the debris and started to serve coffee. The bride's father looks around the room, perhaps glancing at you for a nod of agreement, and decides it's time. He rises to call for silence by clinking a knife or fork against the side of a glass. The chatter briefly falters, but starts up again and he has to clink a second time. The conversation peters out and he's off into his speech. In a few minutes it will be your turn.

Are you ready?

As your heart pounds and your pulse races, you can feel your throat and chest tightening and you wish you could be spared the ordeal. At the same time, you want to do well, make them laugh and make a good impression. Here's what to do.

First, get your breathing under control. It will diffuse your anxiety. Breathe slowly and deeply, pushing out your abdomen and taking care not to raise your shoulders. Fill your lungs and hold the air for a count of two, then breathe out fully. Do that three or four times.

Second, raise your metabolism. Grip the seat of your chair on either side of you and try to lift yourself off the floor. Pull hard, then let go suddenly. Do that three or four times.

Third, run through your opening paragraph. Whether or not you use notes for your speech, you must know your opening lines so well that someone only has to tap you on the shoulder and the words will tumble out. If you have them written down on a card, place the card on the table in front of you and read it without moving your lips.

Fourth, create the 'inner smile' just before you rise to speak. Think of a funny incident involving a child or an animal, an incident that always makes you want to laugh or smile. As you start to smile inwardly, you will notice that your spirits are lifting. As you do so, your face will relax and look friendly, and people will smile at you. That will make you feel more at ease and you will launch your speech with confidence.

As you do that, deliberately start on a lower note than you were about to. Address the clergyman or official who conducted the wedding ceremony, the bride's parents, and the rest of the guests:

Reverend/Father/Mister Smith, Mr and Mrs Brown (bride's parents), ladies and gentlemen.

Then deliver your planned opening paragraph. Do not apologise for yourself, for your speech, or for anything else. Take charge of the 'platform', and take your time.

In the accepted tradition, I have the honour of replying on behalf of the bridesmaids/matron of honour. (pause: one, two) So let me start by thanking you (bride's father) for those kind words.

Delivery

Let's now consider the essentials of **delivery.** As this book is just about the best man's speech and not a public speaking manual, I shall keep these notes to a minimum – a single portion, so to speak. (If you are interested in developing your speaking skills even further, you will find these points expanded in greater detail in one of my other books, *Stand and Deliver: Leave Them Stirred Not Shaken.)*

Stance

Ideally, do not stand behind a table, but come out into the open and let them all see the whole of you. Stand with your feet the width of your shoulders apart, with one foot slightly ahead of the other, and the weight forward so you are more on the balls of your feet than the heels. In this position you will feel poised for action, and you will look good.

Use of notes

It's all right to have notes. Ideally, the speech should be short enough to learn by heart, but it's fine to use cards either as prompts or as security. See Chapter 6 for help in producing speaker's notes. My concern in this chapter is to guide you in using those notes.

When you are not looking at the cards, you can hold them in one hand, with your forearm at waist level. But when you need to consult them raise them to about the level of your chin so that you can glance at the notes without dropping your head. To maintain eye contact with your audience, you must keep your head up, so glance at the notes (don't read them) and resume eye contact with the folks in front of you.

Projecting your voice

If you cannot be heard at the back, they will start fidgeting and even talking among themselves, so speak up. Address the people sitting at the furthest corners of the room.

If you have a voice that does not normally carry, practise increasing its power with this simple exercise:

- first place your forefingers along your upper lip and hum, mmmmmmmm
- feel the vibration coming through your teeth and gums
- next hum: mmmmm nnnnnn mmmmmmm nnnnn
- now say eeeeeee mmmm eeeeeeee and try to maintain the vibration
- once you have mastered that, try mmmmm aaaahhhh mmmmm.

If you can maintain the vibration throughout, you are resonating properly. That means your voice is bouncing off the front teeth (which are hard) and not at the back of your throat, which is soft.

Now practise parts of your speech, hitting the end consonant of each syllable:

Ladee**zzz** an**d** ge**nn**-ti**ll**-me**nn.**

Do only a short phrase or two at a time, or it will drive you mad, but you will find that it will make you much easier to hear and understand from a distance. Prove it to yourself by placing a tape recorder as far away from you as possible and delivering your speech.

Using a microphone

If you have a microphone available, use it, even if you have a strong voice. At a wedding reception there will always be background noise, and the bodies in the room will also absorb a lot of the sound you make. People will therefore miss the endings of sentences, when you drop your voice, and many of your conversational 'asides' and quips, which are usually delivered more softly than your prepared text.

I once gave a demonstration speech to about 50 Americans in Texas. Because I have a strong, carrying voice, I declined the microphone, forgetting that they were going to have some difficulty with my British accent anyway. An elderly lady sitting at the back told me later that I would do fine once I had improved my English pronunciation! However, a couple of my colleagues also told me that they had missed the endings of some of my sentences. The microphone allows you to speak with vocal variety and still be heard.

A stand microphone is better than a handheld one, and you should speak about nine inches away from it. That's about the length of a man's span. Spread the fingers of one hand and place the tip of your thumb against your lips, as though you were blowing a trumpet. The microphone should be no closer than the tip of your little finger.

Drama

The folks out there have been looking forward to your speech. You are the cabaret. So inject some drama into your delivery. Take your time as you tell your stories, and pause for dramatic effect. No one is timing your speech, and you have the floor!

> I considered speaking without notes, (pause) but I didn't think you could cope with the feeling of impending doom! (pause) What's more, I didn't want to be like the actor in the classic story: the actor who had a one line part in a major West End production. (slower) All he had to say was, (pause) 'Hark! (pause) I hear the cannon's roar.' (pause)

All day and all week he went around muttering to himself that one line, (louder and slower) 'Hark! I hear the cannon's roar.'

Opening night arrived, and the actor was ready for his big moment. (pause, then quicker) He heard his cue and opened his mouth to speak, when there was an almighty bang, (pause) and he said, 'Bloody hell, what was that?'

Vocal variety

1. Speak with conviction and energy
    – each speech can expend as much energy as a full day's work.

2. Be focused
    – facts tell, feelings sell!

3. Make it a performance
    – use drama, images, visual aids.

4. Be distinctive
    – make it memorable
    – put your personal mark on it.

5. Use vocal variety
    – entertain and surprise them
    – keep them interested.

6. Have empathy
   - talk to them, not at them
   - don't fear personal contact
   - smile: give them a reason to like you.

7. Maintain good eye contact
   - one friendly face at a time.

8. Show what you mean
   - use gestures and positive body language.

9. Stand tall and balanced
   - stay centred, walk with a purpose.

10. Serve the audience's needs
    - offer information, entertainment, involvement.

Finally, **PRACTISE, PRACTISE, PRACTISE!**

Anecdotes

Choosing wisely

A woman came out of her house and saw three old men with long white beards sitting in her front yard. She did not recognize them. She said 'I don't think I know you, but you must be hungry. Please come in and have something to eat.'

'Is the man of the house home?,' they asked.

'No,' she replied. 'He's out.'

'Then we cannot come in,' they replied.

In the evening when her husband came home, she told him what had happened. 'Go tell them I am home and invite them in!'

The woman went out and invited the men in.

'We do not go into a house together,' they replied.

'Why is that?' she asked.

One of the old men explained: 'His name is Wealth,' he said pointing to one of his friends, and pointing to another one, 'he is Success, and I am Love.' Then he added, 'Now go in and discuss with your husband which one of us you want in your home.'

The woman went in and told her husband what was said. Her husband was overjoyed. 'How nice!!,' he said. 'Since that is the case, let us invite Wealth. Let him come and fill our home with wealth!'

His wife disagreed. 'My dear, why don't we invite Success?'

Their daughter-in-law was listening from the other

corner of the house. She jumped in with her own suggestion: 'Would it not be better to invite Love? Our home will then be filled with love!'

'Let us heed our daughter-in-law's advice,' said the husband to his wife. 'Go out and invite Love to be our guest.'

The woman went out and asked the three old men, 'Which one of you is Love? Please come in and be our guest.'

Love got up and started walking toward the house. The other two also got up and followed him. Surprised, the lady asked Wealth and Success: 'I only invited Love. Why are you coming in?'

The old men replied together: 'If you had invited Wealth or Success, the other two of us would've stayed out, but since you invited Love, wherever he goes, we go with him. Wherever there is Love, there is also Wealth and Success!'

* * * * * * * *

Darwin Awards for Idiocy

These awards are given each year to acknowledge (the remains of) that individual, who through single-minded self-sacrifice, has done the most to remove undesirable elements from the human gene pool.

1st runner-up. Doctors at Portland University Hospital said an Oregon man shot through the skull by a hunting arrow is lucky to be alive and will be released soon from the hospital. Tony Roberts, 25, lost his right eye during an initiation into a men's rafting club, Mountain Men Anonymous (probably known now as Stupid Mountain Men Anonymous) in Grant's Pass, Oregon.

A friend tried to shoot a beer can off his head, but the arrow entered Roberts's right eye. Doctors said that had the arrow gone one millimetre to the left, a major blood vessel would have been cut and Roberts would have died instantly. Neurosurgeon Dr Johnny Delashaw at the University Hospital in Portland said the arrow went through eight to 10 centimetres of brain with the tip protruding at the rear of his skull, yet somehow managed to miss all major blood vessels. Delashaw also said that had Roberts tried to pull the arrow out on his own he surely would have killed himself.

Roberts admitted afterwards that he and his friends had been drinking that afternoon. Said he, 'I feel so dumb about this.' No charges have been filed, but the Josephine County district attorney's office said the initiation stunt is under investigation.

The winner. The (late) John Pernicky and his friend, the (late) Sal Hawkins, of the great state of Washington, decided to attend a local Metallica concert at the George Washington amphitheatre. Having no tickets (but having had 18 beers between them), they thought it would be easy to 'hop' over the nine foot fence and sneak into the show. They pulled their pickup truck over to the fence and the plan was for Mr Pernicky, who was 100 pounds heavier than Mr Hawkins) to hop the fence and then assist his friend over. Unfortunately for (the late) Mr Pernicky, there was a 30-foot drop on the other side of the fence. Having heaved himself over, he found himself crashing through a tree. His fall was abruptly halted (and broken, along with his arm) by a large branch that snagged him by his shorts.

Dangling from the tree with a broken arm, he looked down and saw some bushes below him. Possibly figuring the bushes would break his fall, he removed his pocket knife and proceeded to cut away his shorts to free himself from the tree. He dropped into the holly bushes below, scratching his entire body. In the process, a branch penetrated his rectum and his knife stabbed his thigh. His friend, Mr Hawkins, then attempted a rescue by throwing him a rope. He tied the other end to the pick-up truck, intending to haul Mr Pernicky to safety. Unfortunately, he put the truck into reverse gear. The truck crashed through the fence and fell on Mr Pernicky, killing him instantly and throwing Mr Hawkins to his own death as well.

* * * * * * * *

The accident

A middle-aged woman had a heart attack and was taken to the hospital.

While on the operating table she had a near-death experience. Seeing God, she asked if this was it. God said, 'No, you have another 43 years, 2 months and 8 days to live.'

Upon recovery, the woman decided to stay in the hospital and have a facelift, liposuction, breast augmentation, tummy tuck, etc. She even had someone come in and change her hair colour. Since she had so much more time to live, she figured she might as well make the most of it.

She got out of the hospital after the last operation, and while crossing the street was struck down by an ambulance speeding to the hospital.

Arriving in front of God, she demanded, 'I thought you said I had another 40 years?'

God answered, 'I didn't recognize you.'

* * * * * * * *

If you love something, set it free.

If it comes back, it will always be yours.

If it doesn't come back, it was never yours to begin with. But, if it just sits in your living room, messes up your stuff, eats your food, uses your telephone, takes your money, and doesn't appear to realize that you had set it free... You either married it or gave birth to it.

* * * * * * *

A woman came home to find her husband in the kitchen, shaking frantically with what looked like a wire running from his waist towards the electric kettle. Intending to jolt him away from the deadly current she whacked him with a handy plank of wood by the back door, breaking his arm in two places. Until that moment he had been happily listening to his Walkman.

* * * * * * *

Men and women compared

Nicknames: If Laura, Suzanne, Debra and Rose go out for lunch, they will call each other Laura, Suzanne, Debra and Rose. If Mike, Charlie, Bob and John go out, they will. Affectionately refer to each other as Fat Boy, Godzilla, Peanut-Head and Scrappy.

Eating out: When the bill arrives, Mike, Charlie, Bob and John will each throw in £20, even though it's only for £32.50. None of them will have anything smaller, and none will actually admit they want change back. When the girls get their bill, out come the pocket calculators.

Money: A man will pay £2 for a £1 item he wants. A woman will pay £1 for a £2 item that she doesn't want.

Bathrooms: A man has six items in his bathroom: a toothbrush, comb, shaving cream, razor, a bar of soap, and a towel from the Holiday Inn. The average number of items in the typical woman's bathroom is 337. A man would not be able to identify most of these items.

* * * * * * * *

Computer gender

An English teacher was explaining to his students the concept of gender association in the English language. He stated how hurricanes at one time were given feminine names and how ships and planes were usually referred to as 'she.' One of the students raised their hand and asked, 'What "gender" is a computer?' The teacher wasn't certain which it was, so he divided the class into two groups, males in one, females in the other, and asked them to decide if a computer should be masculine or feminine. Both groups were asked to give four reasons for their recommendation.

The group of women concluded that computers should be referred to in the masculine gender because:

1. In order to get their attention, you have to turn them on.

2. They have a lot of data but are still clueless.

3. They are supposed to help you solve your problems, but half the time they *are* the problem.

4. As soon as you commit to one, you realize that, if you had waited a little longer, you could have had a better model.

The men, on the other hand, decided that computers should definitely be referred to in the feminine gender because:

1. No one but their creator understands their internal logic.

2. The native language they use to communicate with other computers is incomprehensible to everyone else.

3. Even your smallest mistakes are stored in long-term memory for later retrieval.

4. As soon as you make a commitment to one, you find yourself spending half your paycheck on accessories for it.

Acres of diamonds

Several hundred years ago, there was a farmer called Ali who worked very hard for not much more than enough to keep him and his family alive. One day a monk came to his door, begging for food. Ali invited the monk to join his family for their evening meal, and afterwards the monk told Ali stories about the outside world and about the fabulously rich people who lived in cities. They dressed in fine clothes and covered themselves in gold and diamonds. Ali said he did not know what diamonds were or why they made their owners so rich.

The monk looked at Ali for a long moment, then replied, 'A diamond is a drop of sunlight that has been trapped under the ground, where it has solidified. When it is dug up from the ground and polished, it outshines everything around it. It is hard to find, but when you have it, others will pay you a lot of money for it.'

Ali said he wanted one, and he asked the monk where he could look for such a diamond. 'Why do you want diamonds?' asked the monk. 'I want to be very rich,' said Ali. 'I am tired of this hard life.' Ali left his family in the care of a friend, and went on his travels, looking for diamonds.

He went from country to country, looking for those precious diamonds, but his search was fruitless, and soon he had used up all the money he had made from the sale of his farm. In despair, he threw himself into the sea and was never seen again.

Meanwhile, the man who had bought Ali's farm was one day watering his animals in the stream that ran through the farm, when he saw a flash of light in the water. He pulled out a black stone that had a bright eye which caught the light. He took the stone into the house and put it on a table, then forgot all about it until one day the same monk who had visited Ali came by again. When he entered the house, he noticed the black stone and saw it flash in the light.

Excitedly he shouted, 'A diamond! A diamond! Has Ali returned from his travels?' The farm's new owner said Ali had disappeared, but that there were many more such stones in the stream. And that was how the Golconda Diamond Mine was discovered, possibly the richest mine of its time, and the source of the magnificent Koh-i-noor Diamond, which is now part of the British Crown Jewels.

If Ali had looked in his own yard instead of searching the world, he would have found greater riches than he could ever have imagined. May it be that way for you in your marriage.

CHAPTER 11

Jokes and Quotes

Knowing what it means

Today we honour a couple who don't know the meaning of procrastination, who don't know the meaning of apprehension, who don't know the meaning of capitulation, so for their wedding present we bought them a dictionary.

D.I.Y.

He's a great fixer-upper. He believes that for fixing things around the house, nothing is so effective as a credit card.

Repeating gossip

I got a lot of advice about this speech. I was advised to reveal embarrassing secrets, but I said I never repeat gossip...so listen closely now.

Telling the truth

In compiling the stories I'm going to tell you I was guided by the film star, Katharine Hepburn, who said, 'I don't care what is written about me, so long as it isn't true.'

Help with decisions

Someone once said that every busy man should have a wife. Then he won't have to waste time in making up his own mind.

Taking it like a man

No matter what ills befall you, whether you lose your job, get passed over for promotion, or crash your car, take all your troubles like a man – blame them on your wife.

Security

The actress Shelley Winters said, 'Security is when I'm in love with someone extraordinary who loves me back.'

Greater love

Greater love hath no wife than to go out with her husband's credit card, and not use it.

Advice to children

President Harry S. Truman said, 'I have found that the best way to give advice to your children is to find out what they want and advise them to do it.'

Knowing the difference

Winston Churchill said, 'An optimist sees an opportunity in every calamity. A pessimist sees a calamity in every opportunity.'

Wedding vows

A newly wed couple were having their first quarrel. The husband told his wife, 'When we got married the other day you promised to love, honour and obey.' She replied, 'I know. I just didn't want to make a scene in the church.'

Advice for the stag party

One ounce of keep-your-mouth-shut will beat a ton of explanation.

or

One ounce of keep-your-trousers-on will beat a ton of explanation.

Just perfect

My girlfriend likes me just the way I am – single.

Unused opportunities

A bachelor has been described as someone with alibis and girls he hasn't yet used.

Just like Mum

A confirmed bachelor was asked why he had never married. He said that no matter which girl he took home, his mother took an instant dislike to her. His friend advised him to look for a girl just like his mother. Some time later, they met again and the friend asked the bachelor how he had got on. The bachelor said, 'I took your advice. Found a girl who looked like my mother, spoke like my mother, even cooked like my mother, and I took her home to meet my parents.'
'And what happened?' asked the friend.
He said, 'My father hated her.'

Generosity

Be generous. Don't be like my neighbour who said he had given his wife two gifts for her birthday. She said she had wanted something for protection and something to drive. So he gave her a hammer and a nail.

Avoiding disappointment

Expect nothing and accept everything. Then you'll never be disappointed.

Good value

When I told my brother how little a marriage licence cost, he said, 'Bloody hell! That's cheaper than rabbit meat.'

Happiness

The vicar said the groom handed him a thank you note right after the ceremony. It said, 'I want to thank you for the elegant way you brought my happiness to a conclusion.'

Adult education

We've had adult education for thousands of years. It's called marriage.

Baldness

Men spend hundreds and even thousands of pounds on toupees and hair transplants, when what's really needed is more women who like bald men.

Health risk

The greatest cause of heart attacks in men of his age is women of her age.

A good wife

Someone once said, if you want a good wife, find a good mother and marry one of her daughters (from Ken Teal).

Language problems

He's Italian, and he hasn't long been here. So the other day he went with me to a pub to have some lunch. The barmaid came up and asked, 'What'll you have?' and he replied, 'I'll have a quickie.' I had to tell him it's pronounced 'quiche'.

Incompatible

They are incompatible. She has no income and he's not pat-able.

Golfer

I have to warn you that he's not only sexually naive, he's also a golfer. So he thinks that foreplay means you do it with another couple.

Literal minded

His mind moves in straight lines. He's also very obedient and does what he's told. So when he went to the loo and saw the sign that said, 'Wet floor' that's exactly what he did.

In a marquee

Ladies and gentlemen. Welcome to Osama bin Laden's time share.

Obsessions

There is a very fine line between 'hobby' and 'mental illness.'

People who want to share their religious views with you almost never want you to share yours with them.

You should not confuse your career with your life.

No matter what happens, somebody will find a way to take it too seriously.

When trouble arises and things look bad, there is always one individual who perceives a solution and is willing to take command. Very often, that individual is crazy.

Advice for the future

Never say anything to a woman that even remotely suggests that you think she's pregnant unless you can see an actual baby emerging from her at that moment.

Common denominator

The one thing that unites all human beings, regardless of age, gender, religion, economic status or ethnic background, is that, deep down inside, we all believe that we are above average drivers.

Take a chance
Never be afraid to try something new. Remember that amateurs built the ark. Professionals built the *Titanic*.

Epicurus
Poverty conducted in accordance with the law of nature is great wealth.

It is not so much our friends' help that helps us as the confidence of their help.

He who least needs tomorrow will most gladly go to meet tomorrow.

Every desire needs to be confronted with this question: what will happen to me if I achieve it, and what will happen if I do not?

Do nothing in your life which will cause you fear if your neighbour finds out about it.

Necessity is an evil; but there is no necessity to live under the control of necessity.

Making it right
To err is human, to forgive, divine. *(Alexander Pope)*

Do not keep the alabaster boxes of your love and tenderness sealed up until your friends are dead. Fill their lives with sweetness. Speak approving, cheering words while their ears can hear them and while their hearts can be thrilled by them. *(Henry Ward Beecher)*

Noble thoughts

All that a man does outwardly is but the expression and completion of his inward thought. To work effectively, he must think clearly; to act nobly, he must think nobly. *(William E. Channing)*

Never esteem anything as of advantage to thee that shall make thee break thy word or lose thy self-respect. *(Marcus Aurelius)*

Best use of time

Tomorrow's fate, though thou be wise,
Thou canst not tell nor yet surmise;
Pass, therefore, not today in vain,
For it will never come again. *(Omar Khayyam)*

Know the true value of time! Snatch, seize, and enjoy every moment of it. No idleness, no laziness, no procrastination. Never put off until tomorrow what you can do today. *(Lord Chesterfield)*

Here hath been dawning another blue day;
Think, wilt thou let it slip useless away? *(Thomas Carlyle)*

Fortitude

Keep your fears to yourself, but share your courage with others. *(Robert Louis Stevenson)*

It's not life that counts but the fortitude you bring into it. *(John Galsworthy)*

Patience and fortitude conquer all things. *(Ralph Waldo Emerson)*

In the fell clutch of circumstance,
I have not winced nor cried aloud;
Under the bludgeonings of chance,
My heady is bloody, but unbowed. *(William Ernest Henley)*

The chief pang of most trials is not so much the actual suffering itself as our own spirit of resistance to it. *(Jean Nicolas Grou)*

Mind over matter

Our minds have unbelievable power over our bodies. *(André Maurois)*

Courage conquers all things. It even gives strength to the body. *(Ovid)*

A wish

Where there is pain, I wish you peace and mercy.
Where there is self-doubting, I wish you a renewed

confidence in your ability to work through it.

Where there is tiredness, or exhaustion, I wish you understanding, patience, and renewed strength.

Where there is fear, I wish you love, and courage.

Humour

My way of joking is to tell the truth. It's the funniest joke in the world. *(George Bernard Shaw)*

George Bernard Shaw once attended an event on his own. On his return home his wife asked him if he had enjoyed himself, Shaw replied, 'Of course I did. There was nothing else to enjoy!'

Everything is funny so long as it is happening to someone else. *(Will Rogers)*

The marvellous thing about a joke with a double meaning is that it can only mean one thing. *(Ronnie Barker)*

Few women care to be laughed at, and men not at all – except for large sums of money. *(Alan Ayckbourn)*

Men and women

Men have charisma. Women have vital statistics.
(Julie Burchill)

Man's love is of man's life a thing apart.
'Tis woman's whole existence. *(Lord Byron)*

The average man is more interested in a woman who is interested in him, than in a woman – any woman – with beautiful legs. *(Marlene Dietrich)*

A man in the house is worth two in the street. *(Mae West)*

A man is only as old as the woman he feels. *(Groucho Marx)*

My mother said it was simple to keep a man. 'You must be a maid in the living room, a cook in the kitchen and a whore in the bedroom.' I told her, 'I'll hire the other two and take care of the bedroom bit.' *(Jerry Hall)*

Forget your troubles

The best way to forget all your troubles is to wear tight shoes.

The nice part about living in a small town is that when you don't know what you're doing, someone else does.

The trouble with some women is that they get all excited about nothing and then they marry him...

Repartee

This 55-year-old woman was naked, jumping up and down on her bed, laughing and singing. Her husband walked into the bedroom and watched her a while then said, 'You look ridiculous, what on earth are you doing?'

She said, 'I just got my check-up and my doctor says I have the breasts of an eighteen-year-old.' She started laughing and jumping again.

He said, 'Yeah, right. And what did he say about your 55-year-old ass?'

She said, 'Well, your name never came up.'

Life's essentials

The grand essentials to happiness in this life are something to do, something to love, and something to hope for. *(Joseph Addison)*

Happiness

Most folks are about as happy as they make up their minds to be. *(Abraham Lincoln)*

Hesitation

Our doubts are traitors, and make us lose the good we oft might win, by fearing to attempt. *(William Shakespeare)*

Every little counts

It is the greatest of all mistakes to do nothing because you can only do a little. Do what you can. *(Sydney Smith)*

It is better to light one candle than to curse the darkness. *(Confucius)*

Perseverance

Our greatest glory is not in never falling, but in rising every time we fall. *(Oliver Goldsmith)*

No one is ever beaten unless he gives up the fight. *(W. Beran Wolfe)*

When a man's fight begins within himself, he is worth something. *(Robert Browning)*

The lowest ebb is the turn of the tide. *(Henry Wadsworth Longfellow)*

Maturity

When I was a child, I spoke as a child, I understood as a child; but when I became a man I put away childish things. *(St Paul's First Letter to the Corinthians)*

Nature has only a single path and that path is run but once, and to each stage of existence has been allotted its own appropriate quality; so that the weakness of childhood, the impetuosity of youth, the seriousness of middle life, the maturity of old age – each bears some of Nature's fruit, which must be garnered in its own season. Each has something which ought to be enjoyed in its own time. *(Marcus Tullius Cicero)*

Growing old

Grow old along with me!
The best is yet to be. *(Robert Browning)*

I shall grow old, but never lose life's zest,
Because the road's last turn will be the best.
(Henry van Dyke)

Life must be measured by thought and action, not by
time. *(Sir John Lubbock)*

Helping others

That best portion of a good man's life –
His little nameless, unremembered acts
Of kindness and of love. *(William Wordsworth)*

If I can stop one heart from breaking,
I shall not live in vain;
If I can ease one life the aching,
Or cool one pain,
Or help one fainting robin
Unto his nest again,
I shall not live in vain. *(Emily Dickinson)*

Actual exam answers (from American 10-year-olds)

◆ Solomon had 300 wives and 700 porcupines

◆ Queen Elizabeth was the 'Virgin Queen'. As a
queen she was a success. When she exposed herself
before her troops they all shouted 'Hurrah!'

◆ Socrates was a famous Greek teacher who went
around giving people advice. They killed him.
Socrates died from an overdose of wedlock. After
his death, his career suffered a dramatic decline.

♦ The Greeks were a highly sculptured people, and without them we wouldn't have history. The Greeks also had myths. A myth is a female moth.

♦ Moses led the Hebrew slaves to the Red Sea, where they made unleavened bread, which is bread made without any ingredients. Moses went up on Mount Cyanide to get the ten commandments. He died before he ever reached Canada.

♦ The greatest writer of the Renaissance was William Shakespeare. He was born in the year 1564, supposedly on his birthday. He never made much money and is famous only because of his plays. He wrote tragedies, comedies and hysterectomies, all in Islamic pentameter. Romeo and Juliet are an example of a heroic couple. Romeo's last wish was to be laid by Juliet.

♦ Writing at the same time as Shakespeare was Miguel Cervantes. He wrote Donkey Hote. The next great author was John Milton. He wrote Paradise Lost. Then his wife died and he wrote Paradise Regained.

♦ Johann Bach wrote a great many musical compositions and had a large number of children. In between he practised on an old spinster which he kept up in his attic. Bach died from 1750 to the present. Bach was the most famous composer in the world and so was Handel. Handel was half German, half Italian and half English. He was very large.

◆ The nineteenth century was a time of a great many thoughts and inventions. People stopped reproducing by hand and started reproducing by machine. Louis Pasteur discovered a cure for rabbits. Charles Darwin was a naturalist who wrote the Organ of the Species. Madman Curie discovered the radio. And Karl Marx became one of the Marx Brothers.

Institution
Marriage is an institution. But who wants to live in an institution? *(Groucho Marx)*

Durability
I chose my wife as she did her wedding gown, not for a fine, glossy surface, but such qualities as would wear well. *(Oliver Goldsmith)*

Celebrity points of view
I was the best man at the wedding. If I was the best man, why was she marrying him? *(Jerry Seinfeld)*

I was married by a judge. I should have asked for a jury. *(George Burns)*

My parents stayed married for forty years, but that was out of spite. *(Woody Allen)*

Your marriage is in trouble if your wife says, 'You're only interested in one thing' and you can't remember what it is. *(Milton Berle)*

Why does a woman work for years to change a man's habits, and then complain that he's not the man she married? *(Barbra Streisand)*

I wouldn't object to my wife having the last word – if only she'd get to it. *(Henny Youngman)*

I told someone I was getting married, and they asked, 'Have you picked a date yet?' And I said, 'Wow! You can bring a date to your own wedding? What a country!' *(Yakov Smirnoff)*

CHAPTER 12

Traditional and Celebrity Sayings

Irish Sayings

Get on your knees
And thank the Lord
You're on your feet!
May your blessings outnumber the shamrocks that grow,
And may trouble avoid you wherever you go.

May the sun shine all day long,
Everything go right and nothing go wrong.
May those you love bring love back to you
And may all the wishes you wish come true!

Walls for the wind
And a roof for the rain,
And drinks beside the fire.
Laughter to cheer you
And those you love near you.
And all that your heart may desire.

May the sound of happy music
And the lilt of Irish laughter
Fill your heart with gladness
That stays forever after.

May the grass grow long on the road to hell for want of use.

May your doctor never earn a dollar out of you,
May your heart never give out,
May the ten toes of your feet steer you clear of
misfortune.
And before you're much older,
May you hear much better blessings than this.

May your troubles be as few and far between
As my grandmother's teeth.

May your past be a pleasant memory,
Your future filled with delight and mystery,
Your now a glorious moment,
That fills your life with deep contentment.

May your day be filled with blessings
Like the sun that lights the sky,
And may you always have the courage
To spread your wings and fly!

May we live in peace without weeping.
May our joy outline the lives we touch without ceasing.
And may our love fill the world, angel wings tenderly
beating.

May the frost never afflict your spuds.
May the outside leaves of your cabbage always be free of
worms.
May the crow never pick your haystack.
And may your donkey always be in foal.

May the leprechauns be near you
To spread luck along your way.

May your right hand always
Be stretched out in friendship
And never in want.

May the hinges of our friendship
Never grow rusty.

May you live as long as you want,
And never want as long as you live.

May your glass be ever full.
May the roof over your head be always strong.
And may you be in heaven
half an hour before the devil knows you're dead.

Always remember to forget
The things that made you sad.
But never forget to remember
The things that made you glad.
Always remember to forget
The troubles that passed away.
But never forget to remember
The blessings that come each day.

May the road rise to meet you.
May the wind be always at your back.
May the sun shine warm upon your face,

And rains fall soft upon your fields.
And until we meet again,
May God hold you in the hollow of His hand.

May the roof above us never fall in.
And may the friends gathered below it never fall out.

May you have warm words on a cold evening,
A full moon on a dark night,
And the road downhill all the way to your door.

May there be a generation of children
On the children of your children.

May you live to be a hundred years,
With one extra year to repent!

May your neighbours respect you,
Trouble neglect you,
The angels protect you,
And heaven accept you.

May brooks and trees and singing hills
Join in the chorus, too.
And every gentle wind that blows
Send happiness to you.

May you be poor in misfortune,
Rich in blessings,
Slow to make enemies,
And quick to make friends.

But rich or poor,
Quick or slow,
May you know nothing but happiness
From this day forward.

Count your blessings instead of your crosses;
Count your gains instead of your losses.
Count your joys instead of your woes;
Count your friends instead of your foes.
Count your smiles instead of your tears;
Count your courage instead of your fears.
Count your full years instead of your lean;
Count your kind deeds instead of your mean.
Count your health instead of your wealth;
Love your neighbour as much as yourself.

As you slide down the banister of life,
May the splinters never point the wrong way!

Love Quotes

An old-fashioned home blessing:
May your home always contain
Honey for sweetness
Wood for warmth
Salt for health
Money for wealth
Bread for food
And a black cat for luck.

Lilly Tomlin on love:
If love is the answer, could you rephrase the question?

Chekhov on marriage:
if you're afraid of loneliness, don't marry.

The Prince of Conti, a noted rake, when he at last became aware of his failing sexual prowess:
It is time for me to retire. Formerly my civilities were taken for declarations of love. Now my declarations of love are taken for civilities.

T. E. Lawrence on reading Lady Chatterley's lover:
Surely the sex business isn't worth all this damned fuss? I've met only a handful of people who cared a biscuit for it.

C. S. Lewis on desire:
He that but looketh on a plate of ham and eggs to lust after it, hath already committed breakfast with it in his heart

Benjamin Disraeli
The magic of first love is our ignorance that it can ever end.

Gus Kahn
Another bride, another June,
Another sunny honeymoon,
Another season another reason,
For makin' whoopee!

Arnold Bennett – Quotations for Our Time:
Make love to every woman you meet. If you get 5% on
your outlays it's a good investment.

Cole Porter
I get a kick from champagne,
Mere alcohol doesn't thrill me at all,
So tell me why should it be true,
But I get a kick out of you.

Lorenz Hart
The broken dates,
The endless waits,
The lovely loving and the hateful hates,
The conversation and the flying plates –
I wish I were in love again.

E.Y. Harburg, in 'Tennyson anyone?'
In the spring a young man's fancy lightly turns to
thoughts of love;
and in summer,
and in autumn,
and in winter –
see above.

Stephen Fry and **Hugh Laurie:**
I'm afraid I was very much the traditionalist. I went
down on one knee and dictated a proposal which my
secretary faxed over straightaway.

William Shakespeare from *Twelfth Night*:
Many a good hanging prevents a bad marriage.

Samuel Pepys
My wife, who, poor wretch, is troubled with her lonely life.

William Congreve in the *Old Bachelor*
Thus grief still treads upon the heels of pleasure:
Married in haste, we may repent at leisure.
Some by experience find those words misplaced:
At leisure married, they repent in haste.

John Dryden
Here lies my wife; here let her lie!
Now she's at peace and so am I.

Henry Fielding in *Tom Jones*
His designs were strictly honourable, as the phrase is;
that is, to rob a Lady of her fortune by way of marriage.

Samuel Johnson – On a second marriage:
The triumph of hope over experience.

Lord Byron
I have great hopes that we shall love each other all our lives as much as if we had never married at all.

Samuel Taylor Coleridge
The most happy marriage I can picture or imagine to myself would be the union of a deaf man to a blind woman.

George Meredith 1859
Kissing don't last: cookery do!

Punch **1880**
Bishop: Who is it that sees and hears all we do, and before whom even I am but as a crushed worm?
Page: The Missus, my lord.

Benjamin Disraeli
No man is regular in his attendance at the House of Commons until he is married.

I have always thought that every woman should marry, and no man.

Punch **1885**
Wife of two years standing: Oh yes! I'm sure he's not so fond of me as at first. He's away so much, neglects me dreadfully, and he's so cross when he comes home. What shall I do?
Widow: Feed the brute!

Lord Russell, the Lord Chief Justice, was once asked by a lady what was the maximum punishment for bigamy:
Two mothers-in-law.

George Bernard Shaw

Marriage is popular because it combines the maximum of temptation with the maximum of opportunity.

When two people are under the influence of the most violent, most insane, most delusive, and most transient passions, they are required to swear that they will remain in that excited, abnormal, and exhausting condition continuously until death do them part.

A.P. Herbert: *Misleading Cases*

It is probably no mere chance that in legal textbooks the problems relating to married women are usually considered immediately after the pages devoted to idiots and lunatics.

H. L. Mencken

Bachelors know more about women than married men. If they did not know they would be married too.
No matter how happily a woman may be married, it always pleases her to discover that there is a nice man who wishes she were not.

Zsa Zsa Gabor

A man in love is incomplete until he has married. Then he's finished.

Woody Allen

My wife was an immature woman...I would be in the bathroom, taking a bath, and my wife would walk in whenever she felt like it and sink my boats.

Dorothy Parker to another long-suffering wife:
Don't worry, if you keep him long enough you'll come back in style.

Harold Nicolson:
The great secret of the successful marriage is to treat all disasters as incidents, and none of the incidents as disasters.

Evelyn Waugh:
All this fuss about sleeping together. For physical pleasure I to go to my dentist any day.

Mae West:
It's not the men my life that counts – it's the life in my men.

Marriage is a great institution, but I'm not ready for an institution yet.

Love conquers all things – except poverty and toothache.

Mrs Patrick Campbell:
It doesn't matter what you do in the bedroom as long as you don't do it in the street and frighten the horses.

Alan Ayckbourn in *The Bedroom Farce*:
My mother used to say, Delia, if S-E-X ever rears its ugly head, close your eyes before you see the rest of it.

CHAPTER 13

Sample Toasts: Beginnings, Middles and Endings

Whether you make a long speech laced with amusing anecdotes, or simply propose a toast, the decision is yours to make. If you choose the latter course, here are a few sample ideas to get you started. Just remember, the toast should always end with a short and simple cry that all the guests can repeat, such as: 'The bride and groom!'

Some best men ask, 'Do I *have* to give a speech?' The short answer is, 'Yes!' The long answer is, 'Absolutely!' You have got to try, and you will usually have the time to prepare and practise a speech that, at least, covers all the basics. In this chapter, you will find some examples of shorter speeches, and you can mix and match the beginnings and endings, filling the middle with appropriate stories.

Let's start by looking back in time, so see how the whole business of 'toasting' began.

How toasts began

Theory No. 1: There are a number of possible explanations of the practice of toasting, starting with the suggestion that **primitive tribes** would sprinkle a few drops of drink on sacrificial altars to please the hunting gods. This amounted to dedicating the meal or feast to the gods, and in time the dedication took the form of collectively raising the cup or goblet, much as we do today, and saying the name of the god or person being honoured.

Theory No. 2: Another story, according to historian **Paul Dickson**, is that it originated in **Bath, England**, in the year 1709, when a lady who was celebrated for her great beauty was spotted by an admirer bathing in public. He filled a cup with her bath water, dropped in a piece of spiced toast, in the accepted fashion, and drank the water.

Another admirer followed suit, but as he did not fancy drinking the bath water, he offered to eat the toast in her honour.

Theory No. 3: However, the most likely story is that toasting originated in **medieval France**. At a banquet, it was the custom for the menfolk to pass around a goblet of wine, into which a piece of spiced toast had been placed. Each man would repeat the name of hostess or the principal lady guest and take a sip of the wine. When, finally, the goblet reached the lady herself, she would eat the piece of toast and sip the wine which had been flavoured by the toast and blessed by the repeated mention of her name.

In time, the piece of toast was *replaced by a short speech* in honour of the subject of the toast. Its function is specifically to acknowledge and honour the named person or persons in a formal way, and to include the whole assembled company in the process.

Over the years it became known as the signal for drunken and riotous behaviour, so that several monarchs, including Maximillian, Charles the Great, Charles V and Louis XIV, declared the practice illegal. Even the State of Massachusetts in the US, outlawed the custom in colonial days, but no one took any notice, and the law was repealed after eleven years.

Often, people touch glasses when responding to a toast. It's a sign of trust. You see, in the distant past, people were forever bumping each other off. Poison was a preferred means of execution, especially in a goblet of wine or mead, so a guest was always apprehensive about the drink he was being offered.

To allay such fears, the host would pour some of the guest's drink into his own glass or goblet, and drink it to prove that it was safe. However, to show that he trusted his host, a guest would just pick up his glass and touch his host's glass with it, without actually pouring any of his drink. This act of trust signified a bonding that is still part of today's clinking of glasses in a toast.

In North America, on formal occasions, the preference is for the glass to be raised in the right hand, with the right arm straight from the shoulder. This custom derives from the days when everyone walked around with swords and daggers about their persons, and you were never entirely sure if, when an arm was extended in your direction, the hand would be holding a dagger with evil intent. The arm held straight from the shoulder was to indicate that there was no concealed weapon, and that the toast was being proposed with sincerity.

* * * * * * * *

Some sample toasts

Here's a shortcut to preparing a toast.

As I've said, a toast is a mini speech, and therefore it has the usual three parts: a beginning, a middle and an end. I've provided three typical examples for each of the three sections. All you have to do is mix and match, changing the details to suit the occasion.

Step 1: Pick a beginning

A. I would now like to propose a toast to the happy couple. They seem more in love with each passing day, as suited as two halves of a fresh avocado pear, and as well-matched as a pair of bookends.

B. Let me start by thanking Mr and Mrs_____ (bride's parents) for allowing us all to share in this very important occasion in their lives, the marriage of their lovely daughter, (name). Let me also thank (the groom) for his generosity of spirit in finally acknowledging that I am the best man.

C. It is my privilege and pleasure to respond on behalf of the maid of honour/bridesmaids. As this is a rare opportunity to speak while the lovely lady/ladies sit(s) silently, I shall try to do justice to the occasion and to her/them.

* * * * * * * *

Step 2: Pick a middle

A. Look back in time. Look back to the idyllic days of your youth (if you can remember that far back!) and as you do, you will recall the highlights that brought you happiness. The day you passed your driving test...the first time you rode a bicycle without falling off...that first kiss when you thought your heart would burst out of your chest...your favourite puppy...the day you won the egg and spoon race at school. And think about the landmark events that marked your adult life, shaping you and making you the person you are today. One day, (groom and bride) will look back on their lives, and I hope that this day will stand out like a beacon, signalling the start of a richly rewarding life together.

B. I was talking to (the groom) this morning, as we were waiting for (the bride) to arrive for the wedding ceremony, and I asked him if he was nervous. 'No, no!' he said, 'I'm quite relaxed.'

'Then how come,' I said, 'how come I found these in the toilet?' (Produce two bricks from a props box.)

Of course he was nervous. Even I am nervous. He told me that if I did a good job today he would recommend me to both his friends. So let me tell you a bit about him and how we came to be friends.

C. This is one of those three hankie occasions when we celebrate the commitment of two people to each other in the presence of those who care most about them. It is one time when it is not only acceptable but even expected that we – and especially I – should be sentimental about them. We live in temporary times. Everything is temporary. Consumer durables are no longer durable. Companies that once were household names disappear overnight. Relationships come and go, and commitment is as rare as an ice cream in the Sahara. Even marriage is no longer a prerequisite for starting a family. So let us celebrate the decision of (groom and bride) to commit to each other in the traditional way through marriage.

* * * * * * * *

Step 3: Pick an ending

A. So let us congratulate Brian and Jane for taking this significant step, and let us wish them all happiness from this day forward. Ladies and gentlemen, please rise and join me in drinking a toast to the bride and groom. The toast is: **The bride and groom**.

B. I was dry when I stood to make this speech, and my throat is even drier now. It seems to be urging me to have a drink, and the best excuse for that is to drink a toast to the bride and groom. Ladies and gentlemen, will you stand and join me? The toast is: **The bride and groom**.

C. Let me tell you, Brian, you are a very lucky fellow. You, Jane, are beautiful, gracious and kind to undeserving males. But I wish you both well, and may all your troubles be little ones. So I raise my glass to honour you with a smile in my heart, and I ask you all, ladies and gentlemen, to do likewise. Please rise and drink a toast to the lovely bride and her lucky groom. The toast is: **The bride and groom**!

* * * * * * * *

Here's to the prettiest, here's to the wittiest,
Here's to the truest of all who are true;
Here's to the neatest one, here's to the sweetest one,
Here's to them all in one – here's to you!
(*Groucho Marx*)

* * * * * * * *

To the bride's parents
(when they have toasted the bridesmaids)

Thank you, Bob and Muriel, for those kind words. It is my privilege to respond on behalf of the lovely bridesmaids, and I must say I agree with you that they look sensational. I am in the fortunate position of not only being their champion, but of also being able to claim the first dance with all of them. So on behalf of these lovely ladies, and myself and all the people here today, let me thank you for arranging this wonderful party and inviting us to join you in celebrating Jane's marriage to Brian. Ladies and gentlemen, please fill your glasses and rise to drink a toast to our hosts, Bob and Muriel. The toast is: **Bob and Muriel**!

* * * * * * * *

When there are no bridesmaids

As best man I claim the right to propose a toast. First, let me say how honoured I feel to be included in this select gathering. I'm sure, you all feel that way too. I suppose we are the closest relatives and friends of Jane and Brian, and I know we all hold them in the highest regard. When Brian asked me to be best man at his wedding, I was thrilled. Not because I had to make a speech, because frankly I would have preferred a slow roasting over burning coals, but because he is such a lovely fellow and a wonderful friend. That's why he was able to persuade the beautiful Jane to marry him and put an end to his bachelor ways. I know they are right for each other, and that they will make each other very happy. So, ladies and gentlemen – friends – let us mark this significant occasion by drinking a toast to their health, their wealth and their eternal happiness. Please fill your glasses and rise. The toast is: **Brian and Jane**.

* * * * * * * *

CHAPTER 14

Mixed Marriages

This chapter is not intended to be an detailed guide to all mixed weddings – black/white, Jewish/Christian, Catholic/Protestant, foreign/English – because that would be a whole book. Rather, it is a prompt to be sensitive to racial, religious and cultural differences. The ceremonies themselves are different, and so are the roles of the principal players. If, for example, you were attending a traditional Indian wedding, you would not expect to make a best man's speech, unless there were a western-style reception afterwards.

It is essential, however, in every mixed wedding to get advice from those who have had the experience before, and that usually means finding the relevant support group. One example is the Northern Ireland Mixed Marriages Association (NIMMA), which was set up in 1974 at Corrymeela to collect and co-ordinate the experiences of those who had married across the Christian divide.

NIMMA's declared objectives are to:

1. Act as a mutual support group.
2. Provide advice and information to anyone who contacts them through their office.
3. Help the clergy to understand the concept and practicalities of inter-church marriage.

4. Influence the local community's attitude to mixed marriages.

The global neighbourhood

Cross-cultural and inter-racial marriages are growing. Increasing numbers of (mainly) younger people are crossing the traditional barriers of religion, language and ethnicity. Despite the corresponding liberalisation of society's attitudes, there may always be an emotional resistance within the family circle, based on the idea that the intended spouse is 'not one of us'. Even though acceptance may have been gained by the time the wedding day dawns, there could be a lingering reluctance in somebody's heart. So be careful in what you say, and do not risk making insensitive racial jokes. The best man's brief does not include a mission to alter attitudes.

Mixed marriages are very much more accepted today than they ever were before, and it's not such a big deal, but the cultural differences do need to be acknowledged. The ceremonies themselves remain traditional and different (Jewish, Muslim, Hindu, Chinese, African...) but the reception can be the same as any Christian wedding. You may therefore find yourself with normal best man duties (including the speech) even though you may not have been involved in the ceremony.

Here are a couple of sample speeches for you to use as models, to adopt or adapt as necessary.

Sample Speech A:
Jewish bride, Afro-Caribbean groom

(Note: This is equally applicable if the bride is Christian, Hindu, Muslim...)

Rabbi Goldberg, Mr and Mrs Cohen, ladies and gentlemen.

I am conscious of the great honour and responsibility given to me today, as I rise to speak to you. Because my role in today's proceedings has been much more than that of a master of ceremonies or a facilitator, to use a business term. I feel that mine is a diplomatic role, and that I must help to form a bridge between the two cultures/nations represented by the bride and groom and their respective families.

And yet, it is obvious that I shall not need to apply very much diplomacy, because no matter what your cultural background might be, you will surely appreciate the bride's fairy tale beauty. Indeed, the wedding itself has been the climax of a wonderful romance, and I'm sure we all wish the bride and groom a future that is as magical and happy as any fairy tale, a future in which they live happily ever after.

Although Denton and Rachel come from such different backgrounds, they have much in common. Moreover, their cultural differences will enrich each other's lives and the lives of their children. Their marriage has brought together their respective families, as you can see when you look around this room. Perhaps it will make a contribution to a greater understanding and acceptance of cultural differences in this country. Knowing Denton and Rachel, as I do, I feel sure they would want that to happen.

Actually, I've known Denton for many years. We went to the same school, which is probably why he asked me to be his best man. And, as I was researching the role of best man, I was struck by the irony of someone like Denton, with his Afro-Caribbean background, adopting a medieval European custom like the appointment of a best man.

Still, he took that decision, and here I am, the lucky holder of a traditional privilege, and glad of the chance to say nice things about one of the best friends I have ever had . . .

* * * * * * *

Sample Speech B:

Father Gallagher, Mr and Mrs Smith, Brian and Anna-Maria, ladies and gentlemen.

Every country has certain things that identify its own particular culture: its customs, its food, its language. Those are the things that make it different from other countries. But there is one thing that is common to all countries. It is the language of love. The language of love transcends national differences, it wipes out national borders more surely than the Euro, and it unites a man and a woman in marriage, as we have seen today.

Today we have come together, not to deal with differences, but rather to celebrate the coming together of two young people from very different cultures. Brian is Scottish Presbyterian, Anna-Maria is a Catholic from Italy, and Father Gallagher is from Ireland. I myself am a common-or-garden Anglican from London. And, I suspect, most of you are 'don't knows' with complex ancestries.

Yet, here we are, celebrating the marriage of Brian and Anna-Maria in much the same way as marriages are celebrated all over the world. With food and drink. With music. By getting all dressed up. And with hope in our hearts that the bride and groom will be happy, raise children, and pass on their values to those children.

In a way, the children of mixed marriages are fortunate. They can benefit from two cultures, and perhaps even from two languages. They have a headstart in tolerance simply because they grow up with difference. They have relatives in two camps, relatives whose lifestyles and customs are very different from one another's, and very different from the norm in this country. That reminds me of the song that swept the country a few years ago, and even featured in a TV commercial for Coca Cola. That song was, 'I'd like to teach the world to sing in perfect harmony.'

And that's the theme of my message to Brian and Anna-Maria. I'd like to wish them a married life that's in perfect harmony. I've known Anna-Maria only since just before she and Brian got engaged, but I've known Brian for many years...

* * * * * * *

CHAPTER 15

Sample Speeches

Sample Speech 1

This is the first of several full length speeches, to illustrate how to bring in stories about the groom's early days, how he and his bride met, and your role in the mix.

(*Title of clergyman*), ladies and gentlemen, boys and girls. It is my privilege and pleasure to respond on behalf of the bridesmaids. And on their behalf I'd like to thank John for his kind words. I know he meant them all, because John is a man of great kindness.

Let me tell you something about John. He was born at a time of many changes, some of which may have shaped the way he has developed. As you know, he is an airline pilot. That may be because as a young child he was regularly taken by his father to the Biggin Hill air show where he saw Brian Trubshaw flying the Concorde prototype. Yes, that's how long ago it was. A tiny, young John gazing up at the magnificence of the early Concorde, both at the start of their amazing lives.

In those days, John had stars in his eyes. Now he's a star in the skies.

In his school years, he did all the usual suburban things. He was a Cub Scout, then a full Scout. He promised

Akela he would do his best, and his parents dabbed their eyes through the emotion of it all. He went to Scout camps and on school trips to the Lakes, and learned how to live with the smell of other people's socks. He learned how to resolve conflicts within the group when it wasn't possible to go home to Mum and Dad at the end of a difficult day. He learned to share. And that's what has made him the good friend that he is today.

He was a star sportsman too. For a time he was uncertain which way to go because he shone at cricket, at rugby and in athletics as well. He ran for his school and also for the local running club, and won medals for both. But in the end, it was rugby that claimed his allegiance, and not only for the shared experience of communal showers after the game. Nor was it for the togetherness of tackles on the field of play. It was for the test of courage in every game he played.

John took his studies seriously too. He would play hard and party hard, but he always made time for his homework and made sure he had enough rest before an exam.

If all that makes him sound like a goody-goody, I apologise. John is not a goody-goody he's just bloody good at whatever he sets his heart on.

When he first went out to work, he found his own first job, sent off his own application, handled the interview with style, and only told his parents about it when he was offered the job. It was an indication of the entrepreneurial spirit that has made him so successful.

It was as a young entrepreneur that John made his first pile of money, to help pay for his flying lessons. He ran a weekend market stall which he stocked initially by asking all his neighbours if they had any bric-a-brac and other stuff they wanted to give to the charity shop. He offered to deliver the stuff to the charity shop if they would first allow him to choose whatever he needed for his weekend stall. By investing all the money he made in new stock he was able to upgrade the level of his trading and make even more money.

It was about that time that John had a serious argument and lost. The argument was between his car and a local lamppost, and the lamppost won. John was returning from a party one cold and frosty night, when he hit a patch of black ice. The car did a slow motion waltz down the middle of the road, narrowly missing a van coming in the opposite direction, and wrapped itself in warm embrace around a lamppost.

What made it worse was that the car he was driving wasn't John's at all. It was his father's car. And, to make matters worse, it happened well before the age of mobile phones, so John had to go in search of a public phone to call his Dad. And that's not all. When he found a phone, he also found that he had no money, and he had to reverse the charges.

So not only did he crash his father's car, but he made his father pay to receive the bad news as well!

Fortunately, such a reversal was rare, because whatever John attempted seemed to turn out right. And that includes the way he met Margaret.

John and his mates were down at the King's Head, where they would meet to watch England's international rugby matches on the telly. There they were, a bunch of blokes sitting on this side of the bar, and there was a smaller group of girls sitting on that side of the bar, all watching the rugby and getting very excited. One of the girls had a loud, penetrating voice that was impossible to ignore. That was Margaret.

At half time John went over and struck up a conversation with Margaret. Just like that. And she responded. Then he noticed that she had a sports bag by her side, with a squash racket sticking out. Quick as a flash he asked if she'd fancy a game of squash with him. Margaret agreed, and they exchanged phone numbers. Well, it makes a change from, 'Do you come here often?'

Anyway, it was a short hop from squash to squeeze, and soon John and Margaret became an item.

Then came John's next promotion, with a hefty hike in his salary, so he bought a new flat and invited Margaret to move in with him. It was quite interesting how he did that. Ever the romantic, John took Margaret out for dinner one night at one of those fancy places where people go to get engaged, with champagne, soft lighting and sweet music. At the end of the meal there was a sort of birthday cake with sparkling candles and applause from the staff, and then John presented Margaret with a small package.

When she opened it up, she found two sets of keys the keys to John's new flat, and the keys to his car. And when she drank the champagne he handed her, she saw a diamond ring at the bottom of the glass.

The engagement was short, and before long it was time for John's stag night. Now, I know you will all want to hear details of that riotous event, but I am sworn to secrecy. However, I do have some photographs here to prove that John can be very silly when he chooses to do so. Margaret, you have been warned!

I also have some cards from friends and family, some of whom could not be here today. (*Read them out.*)

John and Margaret, if I said that this is the happiest day of your lives, it would suggest that things can only get worse. But I know that things will get even better than they have already been.

John, we have been mates for a number of years, and it has been a honour to serve as your best man, although

I've not quite understood how that squares with the old saying, 'May the best man win'. I wish you a long and happy married life. Woody Allen once said, 'My parents have been together for 40 years... but that was out of spite.' I'm sure that will not apply to you. May your time together stretch into eternity, and may it seem not a day too long.

(The father of the bride usually toasts the couple, but if you are asked to do so, just continue by saying:)

So, ladies and gentlemen, please rise and join me in drinking a toast to the new Mr and Mrs Groom, to wish them a wonderful married life. The toast is: John and Margaret Groom!

* * * * * * * *

Sample Speech 2

This sample speech focuses on the development of the relationship between the groom and the best man, giving an insight into the groom's bachelor ways, and how, at last, he met his Waterloo.

(*Title of clergyman*), ladies and gentlemen, boys and girls. On behalf of the bridesmaids, I would like to thank Ben for those kind words. So let me start by offering him and Jane some kind words in return. These are the kind words sent by family and friends, some of whom could not be here in person today.

(*Read cards*)

I have composed a few words myself to celebrate this very special occasion, and the way I feel about these two very special people. It goes like this:

Ben once was a bachelor swain
Who refused to commit, with disdain.
He swung through the trees
Like Tarzan at ease,
But was finally grounded by Jane.

I met Ben a number of years ago, when we were both at the interesting stage between childhood and adultery. I had just moved to this town from a much quieter environment, and was having difficulty coping with the curious sounds that formed a permanent backdrop to daily life. There was the constant hum and roar of traffic, the distant barking of dogs, the intermittent wailing of sirens and car alarms, and a strange droning that seemed to come from somewhere near.

At first I had trouble locating the sound, which started up most evenings at around eight o'clock and continued unabated for over two hours. Then one evening I plucked up enough courage to venture into the pub next door to where I lived. Now remember, I was new in town, came from a rural background, didn't know anyone in my new neighbourhood, and had heard frightening stories about drunken behaviour in town pubs. I don't know what I expected, but it was probably scenes of violence and/or debauchery.

Well, I wouldn't have minded the debauchery, so I was probably half hoping to find some in the pub. Anyway, I crept in the door, and was surprised that no one took any notice of me. But what did surprise me was that the droning noise was much stronger inside the pub. A moment later I discovered its source. It was Ben holding forth on any and every topic that cropped up. He had words, he had opinions, and he had the self-confidence to put them across in the full expectation that they would be well received. He was, in short, a purveyor of words.

Interestingly enough, he was with a group of people who didn't seem to mind his endless stream of ideas, even when it was plain that he was making it up as he went along. And that was the second clue to this remarkable young man. You may have to battle to get a word in edgeways when you are with him, but he's always good company.

Ben noticed me standing alone, with my pint, on the edge of his group, and he invited me to join them. I did so, and was immediately singing for my supper as Ben welcomed me as the next topic of conversation. He quizzed me about my background, my family, where I went to school, and the games I played. He asked why I had moved there, what I did for a living, even my inside leg measurement. You see, that's another characteristic of Ben. He is quick to pick up a new interest, and quick to make himself as expert as he can on that subject. Well, I was his latest subject, and he must have liked what he heard because we became good friends from that evening on, and instead of listening to the droning noise from inside my flat, I sat in the pub alongside its source and found it a much more enjoyable experience.

That's not to say we always got on. Once I got to know Ben well enough, I had the temerity to disagree with him on the subject of religion. Or, to give it its proper name, football. As you know, football is like a religion for its fanatical followers, and Ben's devotion to Arsenal is nothing short of fanatical devotion. My own allegiance, however, is to Blackburn Rovers. And although the two clubs are not exactly rivals, each excites a similar degree of passion in the two of us. And when Ben extols the virtues of his north London club, to the exclusion of all other contenders, I feel it would be disloyal to my own preferred choice if I did not counter with a tale or two of our own achievements.

On one occasion, the football rivalry became rather heated, and we even descended to a bit of push and shove, with our chins only one inch apart. As we grappled, we tripped and fell to the floor, whereupon we both felt ridiculous and started giggling. We never had a serious falling out again, although our understanding was sorely tested when we started playing squash against each other.

I don't know if you knew this, but Ben is rather competitive. He's an only child, and has always got his own way. So when he plays a competitive sport, he expects to win. Not only that, he expects you to lose. Even worse, he expects you not to mind losing to him. Trouble is, on the squash court, he used to be a menace. He would swing his racket dangerously and rush around the court, getting in his opponent's way and even crashing into the other player. This caused us a few interesting moments especially when I claimed the point every time he made a dangerous move.

However, I believe it was the give and take of our relationship, both on the squash court and in the pub dialogues, that prepared Ben for the ultimate change in his lifestyle – the change that has led to this very day.

As I implied in my opening ode, Ben was a bachelor boy, quite happy to spend his time and his money in any way he chose. No ties, no responsibility, no concessions made to anyone, especially not to any women. And then it happened. He met Jane.

I wasn't present when they met, so my report is second-hand. But I can tell you that the effect was as dramatic as it was unexpected. My sister Becky came down to visit me, and she brought along a school friend for company. We had arranged to meet in my local pub – not the one where I had first met Ben, because I had moved since then, but my current local, and I was late. But Ben was there, and he recognised my sister from photographs I had shown him, so he went up and introduced himself, and she introduced him to her friend, Jane.

Becky said Ben went bright red, his eyes popped wide and his jaw dropped open. He looked like a goldfish choking, and for once in his life he was lost for words. Tarzan had met his Jane. By the time I arrived, he had recovered a little and was showing off a bit, but he had eyes only for Jane.

In the olden days, it used to be the man who would literally sweep the girl off her feet, often actually kidnapping her. That's why he needed a best man to fight off her family while he made good his escape. But in this case, Ben was the captive from the first moment he met Jane.

I promised not to say or do anything that would embarrass Ben today. But I lied. I got in touch with some of his previous girlfriends and asked them to return his house keys, and here they are. (Hold up large bunch of keys.) I told them that their relationships with Ben were now over, because he had found his soulmate. Some of the young ladies were deeply upset, as you can imagine, and I felt obliged to console them by giving them my own telephone number! Anything for a friend...

Ben and Jane, I wish you all happiness, good health and boundless wealth. May all your troubles be little ones.

(The father of the bride usually toasts the couple, but if you are asked to do so, just continue by saying:)

Well, ladies and gentlemen, I know you would want to join me in wishing the new Mr and Mrs Groom a long and happy married life, so please rise and drink a toast to the bride and groom. The toast is: The bride and groom.

* * * * * * * *

Sample Speech 3

This is a speech for the wedding of a trader on the stock exchange, to provide an example of how to develop the background of a high-powered person. It concludes with a toast to the two families that are being brought together by the wedding.

(*Title of clergyman*), Ladies and gentlemen.

It falls to me, as best man, to respond on behalf of the bridesmaids, and to thank James for those kind words. I have some cards and messages to read out, starting with... *(read out cards, making sure you state clearly who sent each).*

Let me now share with you something about James, whom I have known as a colleague and friend for the past six years. I considered speaking without notes, but lost my nerve. I don't want to be like the actor in the classic story: the actor who had a one line part in a major West End production. All he had to say was, 'Hark! I hear the cannon's roar.' All day and all week he went around muttering to himself that one line, 'Hark! I hear the cannon's roar'.

Opening night arrived, and the actor was ready for his big moment. He heard his cue and opened his mouth to speak, when there was an almighty bang, and he said, 'Bloody hell, what was that?'

The role of best man is an interesting one. The very term itself is ambiguous. It doesn't mean best as in 'may the best man win', because in this case the best man is James, not me. Actually, the best man is more like the groom's second in a duel – the fellow who carries the sword and bandages and sees to any wounds that may be inflicted. And what an image that creates! But I'm sure there won't be any crossed swords between James and Elaine. Or any cross words either.

I know for a fact that James regards this marriage as a sort of graduation ceremony in which he surrenders his Bachelor's degree without taking on a Master's. He tells me that he doesn't believe in either of them being the boss, and that is why they will be combining their surnames, and be known as Mr and Mrs Bride-Groom.

When James first announced that he was getting married, he told us, 'I'm taking on a new contract.' Someone immediately asked, 'Are you buying or selling?'

Anyway, we went out to lunch to celebrate. It was a real sit-down lunch, not one of those sandwich-on-the-run affairs that we usually have in the City these days. When the bill came, he picked it up. But I grabbed at it too, saying, 'Let me pay.' We tugged back and forth and eventually I won. But I also lost, because I had to pay for lunch! That little episode reminded me that in life there are two groups of people: the Givers and the Takers. Takers eat better. But Givers sleep better.

James is a Giver. He is generous to a fault in everything he does, even if he is competitive. But that's another story. He is a model of clean living and has been one of the few bachelors in the City without a loose-life notebook. He is also very good at what he does, and is generally reckoned to be one of the best traders in the London Stock Exchange. In fact, he has the ability to become the Top Banana without losing touch with the bunch.

His generosity extends even to disagreements he has with Elaine when they are out driving. Once they had a small difference of opinion about navigation. After a short silence James said, 'OK Elaine, I admit it. I was wrong and you were right.' Now, how many men do you know who would do that? Anyway, it didn't do him any good because Elaine said, 'It's too late. I've changed my mind.'

Another example of James's generosity is his unstinting and even unthinking support of XYZ Football Club. They are so bad, it's embarrassing. One of James's friends is a solicitor who also happens to be a director of the XYZ Football Club. He was handling a divorce case, when the subject of custody arose in the court. The judge asked the child, 'Would you like to live with your dad?' And the child replied, 'No, he beats me.'

The judge asked, 'Would you rather live with your mum, then?' And the child replied, 'No, she beats me as well.' 'Well,' said the judge, 'whom would you like to live with?' And the child replied, 'I want to live with the XYZ Football Club. They don't beat anyone.'

That cannot be said about James. As I said, a moment ago, he is competitive. I suppose you can't be good as a trader unless you have a broad competitive streak. Well, James actually excels at snooker and golf. During one snooker competition, James's opponent approached the ref. and asked if he could play on a different table. 'What's wrong with that one?' asked the ref. And the chap said, 'James is playing on it.'

I'm sure Elaine will have no trouble at all playing on James's table. They have much in common. They share a passion for fast cars, point to point horse riding and clay pigeon shooting, but not for roulette, which seems to be James's only weakness. It's the one activity in which he leaves things to chance.

In his work, in his choice of bride, and even in his choice of home, he has shown superb judgement. James recently bought a magnificent new home for the start of their married life. He told me that it was a two-storey property. The estate agent told him one story when he offered it for sale and a different story after the sale had been concluded. But that's typical of the breed.

Anyway, the pool doesn't leak, the snooker table is level, and the tennis court is free of weeds. In the fullness of time he may even get to fill all five bedrooms. The way things are going for them, when James and Elaine eventually do have kids, and when they buy their first Lego set, I reckon the first thing the kids will build is a tax shelter.

Let me turn briefly to the parents of the couple. To James's parents let me say you have a good bride for your son. And to Elaine's Dad let me say, you're not losing a daughter, you are gaining a bathroom.

To James and Elaine, let me offer a couple of thoughts as well. Marriage is an investment that pays dividends if you put in enough interest. And finally, remember that a kiss is something that brings two people so close together that they cannot see anything wrong with each other.

You have my very best wishes, now and always. It's a privilege to count you both as my friends, and it has been an honour to serve as best man on this special occasion.

Ladies and gentlemen, this wedding not only joins James and Elaine in matrimony, it also brings their two families together. It is the start of new relationships between them, so let's celebrate that as well. Please rise and join me in drinking a toast to the two families. The toast is: The Two Families.

* * * * * * *

Sample Speech 4

When the best man was a woman. This is the actual speech given by Evelyn Ryan when she was the best man. It may be rare but, increasingly, women are being awarded the role of best man. And why not?

Ladies and gentlemen, my immediate reaction to what has been said by the groom is to commend Willie for his wonderful memory. As I rise to this challenge, I thank the lady God that I am only rarely called to account for something I said twelve years earlier. Now you must be wondering why this break with tradition, and I must admit it puzzled me too. It is not so much with the tradition that I have difficulty, but with the lack of updating of the ritual surrounding it.

In the current century we are familiar with romantic notions like wooing and courtship preceding a wedding. Everything is very civilised and we have legal safeguards to protect the rights of both parties. This was not always the case: a bridegroom originally won his bride by carrying her off by force accompanied by a raiding party. To effect the transformation as we know it the bridegroom's raiding companions became a group of young bachelors who attended him at his wedding and became known as groomsmen. However their role remained defensive in case a rival suitor should show up.

By the nineteenth century when the role of the groomsmen had changed to ceremonial attendants, one in
particular began to be singled out as best man and took
charge of some practical arrangements such as safeguarding the ring and paying the priest, tasks which were
deemed too mundane for the groom whose thoughts
might be elsewhere on his wedding day.

Now let's return to the present day and the presence of
the best man and groomsmen remind us that a rival
suitor may be lurking nearby or even amongst us, and if
he makes a move the groomsmen will spring into
immediate action under the leadership of the best man
and defend the bride. The best man is expected to give a
light-hearted speech. It is questionable whether a light-
hearted speech is appropriate following the behaviour I
have just described. He also speaks on behalf of the
bridesmaids who for some unexplained reason are
unable to speak for themselves.

As time has moved on, we can probably conclude that
the likelihood of danger has passed and the traditional
services of the best man and groomsmen will not be
required. I am sure that comes as a great relief to you all,
and also to Willie and Roz.

Willie set this scene with a trip down memory lane, and
as wedding speeches do tend to incline down memory
lane I shall also stroll along that flower strewn path.
Willie and I have something in common that many of

you may not know, and those of you who once knew may have forgotten. We both served an apprenticeship in the pharmacy trade, in a manner of speaking, at a very tender age. My interest was in cosmetics but Willie was developing his entrepreneurial skills. One Christmas the shop was packed and Willie was very busy helping a lady choose a toilet bag as a gift. The choice was between two and the price difference was £5. With total disdain for the commercial needs of his employer, Willie said to the lady, 'As far as I can see the only difference is that there is a face cloth in one and not in the other and who ever heard of paying £5 for a face cloth.' It was as fine an example as you will find of veracity over salesmanship, of truth before profit but not an attitude I would commend to those engaged in wooing or some other persuasive art.

I began by congratulating Willie on his wonderful memory but I also have memories of adventures that Willie and I shared, mainly at Wimbledon Lawn Tennis championships such as the occasion when, as Willie so poetically phrased it, I saw Lendl and fainted. Willie is a terrific guy to go places with because you can be guaranteed a wonderful time. Willie likes to enjoy life and likes everyone else to enjoy it with him. I think that is evident in how he and Roz arranged to entertain us, not only at their wedding reception, but also the day before. I am sure those of you who participated in the golf, canoeing, shopping or sightseeing enjoyed the activity. It has been my great pleasure to have had this opportunity to speak to you today and help dispel the traditional notion that women should be seen and not heard.

I am sure I speak for all the women present and perhaps the others as well, in wishing Roz and Willie a lifetime of happiness together.

Will you now please rise and join me in drinking a toast to absent friends. The toast is: Absent friends.

* * * * * * * *

Index

10 key points, 57, 61
20 top tips, 79

abduction, 17, 18, 56
accent, 74
accident, 113
anecdotes, 58
apple paring, 23

bath, 148
behaviour, 43, 44, 76
boots, 21
brainstorming, 61
breathing, 99, 101
bridal bouquet, 27
bride's pie, 27
bride's speech, 83
bride's veil, 19, 20
bridesmaids, 56, 62, 154
bundling, 28
buttonholes, 34

car hire, 34, 43
cards and messages, 42,
   58, 83
Caribbean, 157
caterer, 33

ceremonial garter, 26
checklist, 32, 33, 41, 95
comparing, 114
computers, 70, 115
courting, 28
cue card, 87, 88, 93, 95

D.I.Y., 119
Darwin awards, 110
delivery, 97, 103
diamonds, acres of, 117
difficult situations, 43
diplomacy, 157
disco, 35, 62
divination, 24
drama, 106
drunken guest, 43

Egyptians, 18
emergency kit, 39, 86

fear, 45
fertility, 27
flowers, 24
formal wear, 31, 34, 86, 94

garter, 26

gender, 115
getaway car, 41, 44, 82, 84
Gettysburg address, 47
gifts, 58, 84, 94
groomsmen, 17, 36
guest list, 32, 36

honeymoon pack, 84
Hook, 65, 67
humiliation, 73

Irish sayings, 136

Jewish, 156, 157
jilting, 73

key points, 57, 61
kidnapping, 17

language, 74
Leap Year's Day, 23
Lincoln, Abraham, 47
love, 109, 128, 140

master of ceremonies, 18, 38, 49
matron of honour, 18, 42, 56
microphone technique, 105

morning suits (see formal wear)
music, 44

nightmare, 45
NIMMA, 155
notes, use of, 103, 106

parents, 52, 77, 153
Past relationships, 72
paying, 36, 85, 91, 92
planning, 33
pomposity, 73
posset, 28
props, 58
punctuality, 72

races, 26
reception, 41
receiving line, 82, 93
register office, 36, 81
rehearsing, 87
research, 37, 53
ring(s), 27, 39, 79, 80, 91, 92
Romans, 19, 20

sequence, 59, 63
shoes, 20
siblings, 37, 51, 52

sixpence, 29
something borrowed, 29
something old, 29
speaker's notes, 66, 67, 97
spiced toast, 148
stag night, 78, 86, 121
stance, 103
stockings, 27, 28, 29
success, 51, 109
superstitions, 22
swearing, 75

table plan, 37
threshhold, 22
throwing rice, 21
toastmaster, 38

toasts, 42, 59, 147, 150, 154
touching glasses, 149
transport, 90
tying shoes, 20

ushers, 40, 81, 91

vegetarians, 37
veil, 19, 20
vocal variety, 107
voice: projecting, 103, 104

wedding cake, 18, 27
wedding ring, 19
witnesses, 40

Other Titles from How To Books

2-4-6-8 How Do You Communicate?, Phillip Khan-Panni, 2001

365 Steps to Self-Confidence, David Lawrence-Preston, 2001

A-Z of Correct English, Angela Burt, 2002

Blank Page to First Draft in 15 Minutes, Phillip Khan-Panni, 2001

Buy Your Home at Half the Price, Maxwell Hodson, 2001

Buying a House, Adam Walker, 2001

Feeling Good, Pete Cohen and Judith Verity, 2001

How to Make Money from Property, Adam Walker, 2000

Managing Your Personal Finances, John Claxton, 2000

The Ten Career Commandments, Rob Yeung, 2002

Toasts and Short Speeches, John Bowden, 2000

Tracking Down Your Ancestors, Dr Harry Alder, 2002

**For comprehensive information on
How To Books' titles visit How To Books on line at
www.howtobooks.co.uk**